HEARTBREAK, MOURNING, LOSS

VOLUME 2: YOUR BRAIN IN LOVE

ALSO BY GINETTE PARIS

—*The Wisdom of the Psyche: Depth Psychology after Neuroscience*. Routledge. London and San Francisco. First edition 2010. Second edition 2015.

—*The Psychology of Abortion*. Spring Publications. 2007.

—*Pagan Grace*. Spring Publications, 1990.

—*Pagan Meditations*. Spring Publications, 1986.

www.ginetteparis.com

HEARTBREAK, MOURNING, LOSS

(SECOND EDITION)

VOLUME 2: YOUR BRAIN IN LOVE

GINETTE PARIS PH.D.

World Books Collective

Heartbreak, Mourning, Loss
Volume 2: Your Brain in Love
Copyright © 2015 by Ginette Paris
Second Edition
ISBN 978-0-692-58785-0

Published by World Books Collective. For information on obtaining permission for use of material from this work, submit a written request to: chevreuil@cgocable.ca

World Books Collective
chevreuil@cgocable.ca

Many thanks to all who have directly or indirectly provided permission to quote their works. Every effort has been made to trace all copyright holders; however, if any have been overlooked, the author will be pleased to make the necessary arrangements at the first opportunity.

Cover: Pierre Guimond

In memory of James Hillman, mentor, friend.

ACKNOWLEDGMENTS

I am grateful to friends, students and patients who gave me permission to use their story of heartbreak as demonstration of the principles of recovery.

I cannot name them, but they will recognize our writing with four hands.

PRAISE FOR GINETTE PARIS' WRITING

James Hillman, Pulitzer Nominee for *Re-Visioning Psychology* and best-selling author of *The Soul's Code*.

[Paris's writing is] emotionally personal, immediately useful, surprisingly original, beautifully deep, this page-turning read also turns the page into a new century of psychology.

What an achievement!

Susan Rowland, author of: *Soul's Jung: a Feminist Revision* and *C.G. Jung in the Humanities*.

For everyone with a heart this book is life sustaining: it affirms the value of heartbreak as integral to the soul's wellbeing.

Superbly uniting the readable and the groundbreaking, at the heart of this weaving of wisdom and science is insight, radical in its practical optimism.

Heartbreak hurts and rips open an otherwise ordered existence. Such gut wrenching pain is here powerfully revealed as not useless nor the dark fruit of simple failure.

Rather the agony of heartbreak is a call to wake up, evolve, learn and grow. Without heartbreak, we are less than human, Paris shows. Each episode of heartbreak, however terrible, is a gift from (unkind but realistic) gods.

Lynn Cowan, author of *Tracking the White Rabbit: A Subversive View of Modern Culture.*

Every once in a rare while a book comes into one's hands that is so satisfying that it's hard to write about it without drenching every sentence in superlatives. ...Paris's jargon-free language invites us to look into the windows of her agile mind without making us feel intrusive... Her formidable intellectual force ... the same dexterity of language as before.

... with a wonderful sense of humor which complements rather than undermines her great love of ideas and life itself.

...I read her books trying to go slowly because it's narrative was so heartening. I still finished it very quickly because it was so heartwarming.

Michael Vannoy Adams, author of *The Mythological Unconscious*, and *The Fantasy Principle*.

Once again Ginette Paris demonstrates that she is quite simply the most original and eloquent of all writers on contemporary depth psychology.

Ernest Rossi, author of *The Psychobiology of Mind-Body Healing* and *Creating Consciousness.*

Ginette Paris boldly steps forth to liberate the human heart recovering from lost love and mourning.

She illustrates her profoundly liberating perspective with many telling, true tales and vignettes of the human spirit in transition.

Maureen Murdock, author of *The Heroine's Journey* and *Father's Daughters.*

A fascinating book, with many layers of meaning. The elegance of her style […] gives us a taste of the awe inspiring mysteries of life and how the present models of psychotherapy

A brilliant look at how the field of depth psychology is enlarging our consciousness.

Jan Bauer, author of *Woman and Alcoholism*, and *Impossible Love.*

An extremely intelligent analysis and critique of the field of psychology today, both within and without academia. […]

Full of brilliant, often poetic, nuggets of wisdom and insight that both startle and satisfy the reader eager for new or original ways to envision psychological reality.

Bob Romanyshin, author of *The Wounded Researcher* and *The Soul in Grief.*

Ginette Paris' book should come with a warning on its cover: Beware:This book is dangerous and difficult because it stirs the depths of the soul even before it touches the surface of the mind.

Paris' marvelously disturbing book does succeed. [...]

Her book has realized the intention, admirably so[...] clearing away the jargon [...] a rare achievement in psychological writing [...] an exercise in homecoming [..] an exercise in anamnesis, work of un-forgetting, which is what makes her book disturbing and worthy of that injunction to beware. [...] this book might be compared to Hillman's ground breaking book, *Re-visioning Psychology*.

TABLE OF CONTENTS

CHAPTER 1

BYPASS YOUR SYNAPTIC BUNDLE OF FEAR

As far as happiness is concerned, its main utility is to make unhappiness possible. We need to form loving and trusting relationships for their rupture to cause us the precious wrenching we call unhappiness. Without the experience of happiness, or even the hope of it, unhappiness would not be so cruel, and as a consequence, would not bear fruits. Marcel Proust[1]

Trust and the possibility of betrayal come into the world at the same moment ... and betrayal, as a continual possibility to be lived with, belongs to trust just as doubt belongs to a living faith. James Hillman[2]

In the past century, there was an unfortunate division between the subject matter of neuropsychology and the lived reality of the mind. This once prompted the neurologist Oliver Sacks to write that "neuropsychology is admirable, but it excludes the psyche"! Happily that situation has now changed. Mark Solms[3]

Our brain is such that it confronts us with primitive reactions when something happens in our environment that has a regressive effect. A loss of love *always* provokes such a regression. You need an objective understanding of the biological aspect of heartbreak; the more you know how your brain becomes dysfunctional, the more you can search for what supports its recovery.

This chapter summarizes the answers from neuroscience to the following questions:

1. What makes love so necessary and so volatile? So luminous and so dark?

2. What is the road from mourning and lovesickness to psychotic breaks, somatic deterioration, murderous behaviors, depression and addiction? How do I avoid it?

3. Which factors make heartbreak a cause of regression or one of evolution?

Science offers a *rational* understanding of the most *irrational* experience: love. It tells us which neurons fire in reaction to which stimulus, how new connections are created, or destroyed. The discoveries in neuroscience have the potential to change the way we practice psychology, educate our children, do politics, consume goods, upgrade medical practices, and also, they old the key to a successful heartbreakthrough.

Recovery from heartbreak happens at all levels of the brain; it involves the highest aspect of human nature (specifically human) yet, it also involves a rewiring of primitive neuronal pathways. The neuroscientist is impotent when it comes to helping you with your heartbreak, and fMRI equipment is useless when you cry in your pillow, yet, intellectual understanding of how the brain makes you love-crazy is crucial to make you wiser, more human in your reactions.

The three actors in your drama

To avoid getting lost in the super-specialized jargon of neuroscience, I am organizing the scientific information in the form of a narrative with three characters: a crocodile, a puppy and a wise human. This formulation may seem as if I am using MacLean's nineteenth-fifty theory of the brain, when he suggested that the brain comprises three parts: the reptilian, the mammalian and the human. This theory has long been surpassed by more refined explanations and is of no use for neuroscientists. Nevertheless, as the neuroscientist Panksepp (1998) writes: "This three-layered conceptualization helps us grasp the overall function of higher brain areas better than any other scheme yet devised."[4]

Neuroscientific theories stay fresh about as long as a bag of onions at the supermarket, but crocodiles, puppies, and humans are immovable categories, suggesting that we sometimes function *like* an unfeeling crocodile or *like* a vulnerable whining pup or *like* a wise (or foolish) human. *Likeness* is the basis of metaphor, the literary device at the core of the humanities. So, let's be clear: I am not proposing to adopt MacLean's theory of the brain, first because it is outdated,[5] and second because my kind of psychology belongs to the humanities, as opposed to neuropsychology, which belongs to science.

MacLean's triune theory of the brain entered the general public awareness in the 1970s and '80s by way of the novelist Arthur Koestler and the popular astronomer Carl Sagan. It was an inspiring narrative because MacLean hypothesized that since we evolved from reptilian brain to mammalian and from mammalian to human brain, our brains would continue to evolve toward forever better brains. Unfortunately, neuroscience soon discovered that our brains sometimes adapt in a way that is a *lessening* of our potential, reminding us that at any time, we, humans, can become stupider and stupider, a less inspiring narrative than that of MacLean, but a sadly plausible one[6].

The risk of regression, stagnation and deterioration is the same at the psychological level. One can *adapt* to the trauma of heartbreak by becoming a fearful, egocentric, passive, depressed individual incapable of ever loving again. Psychotherapists witness that sad phenomenon regularly; some individuals *adapt* to a loveless life by drastically reducing the emotional and intellectual challenges of relationships. Rather than stages of development along a rosy path toward ever better brains, neuroscience now envisions the triune structure (reptilian, mammalian and human) as well as the division along right-brain and left-brain, to be a constant interplay of one structure with the other. Memory and emotion, thought and action, right-left-front-back-center synaptic connections, *all* activity in the brain happens in a network.

For example, it is incorrect to assume that in a situation of heartbreak, one section of the brain is firing neurons, while the other two brains sit back and watch. Although one particular reaction may be dominant, or quicker, the fact remains that the brain is not neatly compartmentalized. Most interestingly, for our purpose, educating yourself can influence which focus dominates[7].   In a poetic description of inner life, Carl Jung called our psyche the *million-year-old psyche* and recommended that we get acquainted with every aspects of it.

Your crocodile psychology: grab, grip, hit

> *"I don't know what got into me when I shot her." (Man doing life in prison for killing his adulterous wife).*

In a computer identity game, our virtual fate depends on which of the characters wins. It is the same with the drama of heartbreak; our fate depends on which of the croc, the pup, or the wise human wins over the other two characters. The victory of the wise human defines a positive outcome, in which winning equals a restored capacity to relate, having known the dark side of love without letting it take all. That victory is impossible if the player ignores the other two actors. The crocodile is a brute but we need his strength, the puppy is a wimp, but an endearing one, and the wise human determines our fate. All three characters, and the neurological reality they metaphorize, must play their role.

The most reactive and primitive part of the brain is called reptilian because we share it with crocodiles, lizards and all cold-blooded reptiles. It comprises the spinal cord, the brainstem, the diencephalons and the basal ganglia. It is responsible for our basic instinctual reflexes of fight, flight, freeze and f... (the four-letter word that indicates a mating that is purely instinctual, as opposed to relational.) The reptilian brain is also called the autonomous nervous system because it is responsible for our mostly unconscious bodily functions of breathing, swallowing, heartbeat, startle reflex, and for the visual tracking systems.

The primitiveness of our reptilian brain tragically shows up everyday in court rooms: a jealous lover coldly kills his rival and then says, "when I found out that she betrayed me with this guy, a blinding rage took possession of me and I began hitting them both"—a typical reaction from the reptilian brain. This kind of blind rage demonstrates the persistence of a set of somatic reactions in *all* of us, which is why we can empathize with Othello. Many individuals are serving life sentences, or living under restraining orders, because of their incapacity to evolve beyond what I like to call their *crocodile psychology*. It is crucial to know that heartbreak *necessarily* activates those primitive reactions; nobody escapes an occasional fit of crocodile rage! As with all of the autonomous nervous system, reptilian reflexes are uncontrollable by the conscious will. However, although no one has *control* over the immediate surge of the impulse, we do have the possibility of control over the behavior that follows this first crocodile reflex. It is called self-mastery, human de-

cency or restrain. If not, the croc wins and you find yourself in prison. End of game!

Philosophers have called the crocodile psychology
by many names: the inherent perversity in humans, the
original sin, our nature as fallen angels, the dark side of
human nature. Neuroscience adds an interesting finding:
we cannot *control* our primitive brain, yet we can *relate*
to it. *Relating* to the crocodile means we must first *acknowledge* the urge to kill, bite, punch, grab. This two-
step process of relating to the crocodile finds a wonderful
demonstration in the Buddhist monk who develops an
above-average capacity to *relate* to the events happening
in his brain. Faced with an instinctual threat—a scorpion
in his shoe, a snake in his path, a moronic driver about to
hit him, the monk's brain, just like anybody's brain, responds with the ultra-quick startle reflex that is the result
of the activation of the reptilian brain. It is the same reflex
that allows the crocodile snoozing on the beach to become
instantly awake when it senses the slightest movement on
the ground. This reflex is faster than the emotion of fear,
which is not as efficient as the ultra-quick reptilian avoid-
ance reflex.

A crocodile does not have a limbic brain, which means
it does not feel what we call fear; it reacts with the same
reflex as a frog catching a fly, a cobra striking at its prey,
your hand moving away from the flame or your feet on
the pedal break. This instinctual reaction is fast and fo-

cused, with no feeling tone. We need this primitive level of reflex for survival. At birth, the doctor checks the baby's reflexes to confirm the proper functioning of this part of the brain. The trained monk first reacts with that same instinctual alert, but the difference between the monk and the average untrained person, is the amount of time it will take for homeostasis to come back and the autonomous system to calm down. When faced with a speeding car about to hit, one should put the brakes on without having to think about it; the reptilian reflex is the most competent in this situation.

The emotion of fear, one that we share with mammals, comes a millisecond later. The difference between the trained monk's reaction and mine, when I see a snake, consists in the monk's capacity to prevent the reptilian reflex from flooding the whole limbic circuitry with the emotion of fear or rage. Heartbreak is the perfect occasion to learn the monk's trick and not end up in court because you impulsively assaulted or harassed the partner abandoning you.

Imagine a woman comfortably seated in a cinema with a friend; she is relaxed, watching a comedy. A man and a woman in the row in front of her are kissing. Suddenly she recognizes the man as her husband, and he is kissing another woman! Immediately her autonomous nervous system, her crocodile, is on alert mode. Her respiration, blood circulation, heartbeat, body temperature, and perspiration begin responding to the threat, just as if the theater were on fire. Popular language reflects this physiological reality: "When I saw them kiss, my heart stopped, my blood froze. I was white (or red, or blue) in the face. I choked. First I was shivering, then I was boiling with rage." These are all somatic disturbances in the autonomous nervous system, regulated by the reptilian brain. It translates as difficulty with digestion, sleep, heart rate, blood pressure, and hormonal flow.

Neuroscientists use the concept of *allostasis*, a word that means maintaining stability (stasis) through change (allo) and is used by medical doctors as a synonym for the basic reptilian stress response. For example, the woman's heart has to beat faster, in other words to *change*, for her body to get the *same* amount of air into her lungs (stasis). Her organism is adapting to the emotional shock, at a cost to her organism. The term "allostatic load" is synonymous with stress; it refers to the cumulative cost to the body when the extra expenditure of energy is too much, or carried for too long, like the excessive wear and tear on a machine.

We deal better with an *acute* and temporary stress, because it can actually stimulate the immune system and help the body react to danger. But a *chronic* stress leads to what psychologists call *burnout* and that my dad used to call *moral exhaustion*. The allostatic load of the woman witnessing her husband's betrayal in the cinema starts with a form of *acute* stress (the emotional shock of betrayal); but if she continues to react with a high level of alarm long after the incident, it qualifies as *chronic* stress and creates increasing somatic damage. Her husband's betrayal makes her literally sick, because she keeps feeling the betrayal with the same physiological arousal. Her body produces the chemical cocktail that comes from the activation of the reptilian brain.

There you are my crocodile!

Statistics about rape and domestic crime demonstrate the frequency with which rejected partners become abusive, men trying to justify their aggression with you-made-me-hit-you and women hiring the meanest lawyer in town with revenge in their heart: "Go for the jugular; I want him utterly broke, even if the legal fees cost me more than the divorce settlement." Hitting or aiming for the jugular is how the reptilian brain fights. Retaliation, revenge, obsessive jealousy, volcanic anger, extreme possessiveness, all are primitive reactions that come with our instinctual makeup.

Since crocodiles can't love, the jealous, controlling behavior of a partner is never proof that you are precious to that person, but rather a measure of his or her crocodilian psychology. Just like a predator tightens its jaws on his dinner, there is a natural urge to secure our grip on the object of our desire: "you are mine, I won't let you escape."

Biochemically, heartbreak triggers those primitive reactions; it is the autonomous nervous system doing its thing, whether we like it or not. Even in the case where the partner dies, the survivor is not spared the reactivity of the crocodile. The anger may be accompanied by a sense of guilt (after all, it is nobody's fault if he or she died) but there is crocodile anger nonetheless, " I need you so much, how dare you die on me!"

The *flight* and *freeze* instinctual reflexes are less dramatic than the *fight* response, but they are equally crocodilian and equally to be expected. *Flight* may take the form of *dissociation* or *denial*: "this is not happening." Or the flight away from the pain may take the form of *idealization* of the lost relationship, where the deceased partner is remembered as a godlike figure. As for the *freeze* response, it may take the form of a depressive stance where the psyche is frozen, inert, stuck in the past. You cannot avoid the instinctual reflexes, precisely because they *are* reflexes, a default setting in the brain. It is crucial to be able to recognize their flare-up in us: "Ah! Here comes my crocodile!"

Although the surge is unavoidable, there is a way *around* the crocodile reactivity. First, the primitive urge must be acknowledged: "I am so angry, I could kill (fight.)"

Or "this is not happening, I can't believe it" (flight.) Or "I am so depressed, I can't get out of bed" (freeze.) Buddhism has a nice name for that psychic discipline; they call it the *witness* posture, which is a way of looking at emotions as one would look at the weather. Witnessing the emotion starts by *naming* it: "Hello Croc! I recognize you with your bad manners!" Giving it a name helps feel the crocodile's surge, feel the temptation to kill, bite, possess. Then, one breathes through it *without judging it*, just as we don't morally judge the weather for being bad. It is nature doing its thing! There is no need for moral condemnation of the croc's reactions. For one, we don't have control over it, and second we need those quick reflexes. The only way to deal with the croc's reactivity is to breathe through it and move to a higher level of consciousness, which is the level where we can avoid acting out our crocodile psychology.

From infancy, we are taught ways to limit the crocodile's reflexes to the briefness that characterizes all reflexes. The best example of our human capacity for emotional regulation can be seen with jealousy. When this dark sentiment fills our heart, we *all* feel the crocodile's viciousness arising. Acknowledge it, name it ("wow! I am so jealous I can barely breathe!") The chemical reaction soon lessens, and you are past the point of automatic reactivity. Nobody is free of jealous feelings, but we all have the capacity to avoid acting on them. This kind of self-discipline qualifies as a moral victory, a *witnessing* of the crocodile. "Hey Croc, I know you are there, but I won't let you dictate my behavior."

Taking revenge, insulting, hitting, shouting at the partner who does not return love belong to our crocodile psychology, the kind of primitiveness that profoundly offends the moral self. To have the *urge* to take revenge is human, but to *act* on it is too much of a concession to the reptilian brain. Revenge is not only morally offensive to our spiritual values; it is also psychologically disastrous because it leaves us with a regressed psyche—if not in prison for life.

I am not suggesting that we should not defend our legitimate interest in a court of law, such as a divorce settlement, or insurance claim. Yet fairness is very different from vengefulness, and it implies a calm and rational mind. Captain Ahab's obsession with taking his revenge on the big white whale is one of the most powerful stories of a person indulging in a crocodile's psychology. Melville's description is beautifully precise: *Ah, God! What trances of torments does that man endure who is consumed with one unachieved revengeful desire. He sleeps with clenched hands; and wakes with his own bloody nails in his palms.*[8]

Your puppy psychology: beg, whine, wait.

Mammals possess a layer of brain over the crocodile: the limbic brain, composed of the hippocampus, the amygdala, and the hypothalamus and periventricular structures. Neuroscientists have demonstrated how the amygdala makes emotions and attachment possible. The amygdala is most of all an emotional alarm and the dispenser of the emotion of fear. It is the keeper of a permanent unconscious memory of every past situation, context, symbol, image, object, odor, sound, or personality type that has ever provoked fear.[9] This primal mammalian level of feeling, based on non-conscious memories, *does not mature*. It remains with us all our life and, as a result, when a situation triggers the emotion of fear, we regress to the psyche of a two-year old. Our limbic/emotional brain is responsible for a repertoire of reactions that are mammalian reactions *and do not mature with adulthood*.

Academic psychologists, who have to fluff their feathers by inventing jargon and copyrighted concepts to get grants, tenure and sell their books, have many names to suggest that the croc and the pup both need our surveillance. One such concept is that of *affect regulation*. It refers to the kind of self-discipline that my parents and teachers used to call good manners, civilized behavior, self-restraint, moral responsibility or sound judgment in the conduct of oneself. This self-restrain does not come from the croc nor the pup, but from a fully developed, culturally trained human brain.

Normally, we begin learning affect regulation in infancy, when Mom urges you to think before you act and not to grab the other kid's cookie just because you want it. This training is a good example of *relating* to our primitive brain: education changes the pattern of neuronal response and humanizes the child. It is very much the old Aristotelian prescription to act well until it becomes a habit and makes you a good citizen, a good friend, a good partner. Aristotle formulation was elegant: *"Excellence is an art won by training and habituation. We do not act rightly because we have virtue or excellence, but we rather have those because we have acted rightly. We are what we repeatedly do. Excellence, then, is not an act but a habit."* A neuroscientist today might say it this way: *when you repeatedly act well it creates a bundle of synaptic connections that become the default neuronal route.*

One of the reasons we can get so attached to our pets is that they offer a good measure of what neuroscientists call "limbic regulation," a kind of bonding that exists between humans and their pets, and between mother and baby. Pets, because they are capable of attachment, mirror our vulnerability, our enduring need for affection, care, play, security, and comfort. The wimpy puppy whining behind the closed door is a perfect demonstration of our acute distress at being separated from the source of protection and affection.

All young mammals protest, howl, cry, and beg when denied access to their mother or owner. For the human adult, whining takes many forms. Love songs are often calls of distress and protest, to which the artist adds poetry and music. Love songs express, in one form or another, the archetypal plea: "Don't be cruel to a heart that's true,"[10] This complaint is repeated over and over by humans of all times, with endless artistic variations. The theme is timeless and universal: without the beloved, the world is a desert. This distress is part of our default settings in the brain, so much do that it is considered by neuroscientists as the first innate manifestation of *anxiety*, the model for all later forms of anxiety in humans as well as animals. We shouldn't be too embarrassed by our wimpy begging for our partner to come back; we are reacting just like a lost pup trying to attract the attention of its mother.

Your regression to a preverbal vulnerability

The memory of early fear of abandonment exists without words and is often called *preverbal* because it refers to memories that form before the linguistic capacity is developed, around eighteen months of age. Given the long history and fierce theoretical debates around the use of the word *unconscious*, many neuro-psychologists have been quick to take their distance from the psychoanalytic tradition and usually prefer to use terms[11] like *preverbal* or *implicit* memory.

As for *procedural memory*, it is a form of memory that is functional from birth: the baby picks a blueberry, bring it to his mouth and never forgets where his mouth is. (Same as riding a bicycle; you have a procedural memory of how to do that.) Implicit memory or procedural memories are opposed to *explicit* memory, specific to humans, which requires verbal capacity and a conscious, *autobiographical* memory: "look mommy, I ate all the blueberries."

However one chooses to call it, the baby, as every mother knows, is born a little mammal with zero vocabulary. What neuroscientists add to the intuition of the mother is a demonstration that although the baby has no words to form a story of the fearful event, yet *all fearful events* are inscribed in the mammalian brain. That is how the colt learns from the mare not to step on snakes, and how the child learns that playing with matches brings out extremely negative emotions in the parent.

The baby doesn't have the vocabulary to consciously think "mommy gets angry when I grab matches", but matches are to the toddler like the snake to the colt. By the same mechanism, we all have a pre-verbal memory that alarms us that the loss of the parental presence is potentially lethal. This primal anxiety comes back when the experience of abandonment is repeated in adult life. We *all* become beggars for love even if we know that it is bad manners to cry in the soup. The crucial difference is that, as adults, we have the means to relate to our brains in a way that won't victimize us.

Attachment theories

I balk at the way some neuroscientists extend the concept of *joy* to rats; I doubt that *grief* in elephants is as complex as human grief; and I object when neuroscientists apply the concept of *empathy* to mice, as if it has the same meaning as the empathy that funds our humanitarian institutions. Scientists use these words because the physiological manifestations are similar for all mammals, and that includes us, humans. Emotions in the mammalian realm bond us with one another in the sense that they regulate behaviors relative to sexuality, parenting, food distribution, cooperation, competition, aggression, and escape.

Even the so called "spindle cells," which were long thought to exist only in humans or in great apes, have been discovered to be present in other mammals. These cells and their location in the brain are responsible for social organization, empathy, and intuition about the feelings of others. I am always moved by accounts of elephants who suffer from depression when separated from their friendly companion; by dogs who let themselves die when their owner dies, by dolphins who bond with the trainer in the zoo.

All this research confirms that a loss of friendship, a loss of the job that deprives you of the habitual presence of your colleagues, a change of location that separates you from your community, all are psychic shocks of more or less gravity. The young of elephants, dogs, horses, bears, dolphins . . . all show symptoms of psychosomatic disturbances when separated from the parent. The clinical category of *character disorder* has been used to describe monkeys who, because of early rejection, become incompetent parents[12] and lousy teammates.

Research on elephants is especially moving because their long life is responsible for the development of a magnificent limbic capacity from which disenfranchised humans could learn a thing or two! For example, elephants seem to know instinctively who needs help, and how to comfort a traumatized member of their herd. They also spend a huge amount of their time, up to one-third of their waking hours, fondling and caressing each other with their trunks, a soothing and bonding activity. We humans might consider imitating those practices, instead of medicating the consequences of our loneliness.[13]

Given that our limbic/emotional brain is responsible for the survival mechanisms we share with all mammals, it explains how a person who just lost his or her most important relationship emits signals of distress similar to those of any other abandoned mammal. Our whimpers and meows, howling and growling may take the form of repeated phone calls, obsessive emailing, waiting and begging; whatever the expression, the state of alarm is chemically identical to that of the abandoned pup or baby.[14] The kitten that can't access the tit, the child who can't find the mother in the mall, and the adult who is separated from the habitual partner, all suffer the same limbic distress. We shouldn't judge ourselves too harshly when we react like a pup that has been kicked out in the cold winter night, crying to be let in. The thing to do is to let that emotion run its course, without judging it.

Cry in your pillow, reserve a room at Heartbreak Hotel and take residence in the Valley of Tears for as long as you need to get acquainted with your poor little puppy self. That sub-personality is the one that makes you believe that being abandoned is a death sentence. If you are not conscious of that layer in your psyche, you are victimized by it; but if you can separate the adult self from the puppy self, then you can treat the misery. "Ah! There you are my puppy, show yourself, don't be shy because I need to see you before I can help you."

Expressions of emotional distress occur only in species that have developed a limbic brain—which is to say, only when a cry for help has a chance of receiving an answer in the form of rescue. The salmon caught in the net doesn't send a signal of distress to its mommy, because the baby salmon has no limbic brain, nor does the mommy salmon; they have no capacity to experience pain or panic. Same for the crocodile: it looks at its offspring being squashed by a bulldozer without any fuss at all! A crocodile's tears are, indeed, not emotional tears, while a kitten's meow demonstrates a limbic capacity to express a distress to which the mother will respond.

When human adults experience separation anxiety, not only is the activity of the brain similar to that of mammals in distress, the *sequence* of reactions is also the same. An abandoned pup, as well as the human baby, first begins to *protest* loudly, which, in the animal world, is an auditory signal for the rescuing parent to locate the lost pup.

Bowlby's classical studies on loss and attachment were the first to incorporate observations from the animal world into theories of psychoanalysis. Although the establishment of Freudian orthodoxy initially rejected Bowlby's attachment theory, his empirical observations later became known for their accuracy. Today Bowlby's work is confirmed by neuroscience and, along with the work of Ainsworth[15] on attachment strategies, has become the basis for the field of *attachment theory.*[16]

What Bowlby called the "protest phase" is characterized by an increase in heart rate and body temperature, and a surge in the levels of the stress hormones (catechol-amine and cortisol.) The effect of catecholamine is similar to that of adrenaline: it raises alertness, as we can see in the hyper-vigilant attitude of a child afraid that dad may be drunk again and hit at any minute. It is the same anxious hyper vigilance that makes us a bit jumpy at a party when we feel somebody is trying to seduce our partner.

That first phase of *protest* cannot last very long before somatic deterioration starts to happen; if rescue does not come, the little mammal slowly loses the strength to howl and moves into a phase that Bowlby called *despair*, a quiet, depressive emotional withdrawal. Beyond despair is another stage, even more dangerous, one that Bowlby called *miasma*. Bowlby's concept of *miasma* defines a physiological state where you give up trying to be rescued; it leads to what he called a *failure to thrive*. The word *miasma* is an interesting one: in ancient Greece it meant a form of *pollution* of the body/soul connection. Reaction to a loss of maternal care, for the young, is so similar to clinical depression that researchers in pharmacology who study the chemistry of depression use early separation from the animal mother to produce depressed experimental rats.[17] They could as well study the brain chemistry of anybody suffering the *miasma* of heartbreak if their subjects could cry in the lab with the same abandon as when they cry on their pillow.

As Bowlby observed, the normal adult couples repro-
duce for each other the same kind of emotional security
as between mother and child. The longer the miasma persists, the more the immune system weakens. As the emotional stress moves from acute to chronic, the learning
centers deteriorate; the young mammal (including human
babies) eventually refuses nourishment, and soon dies.

We now know the mechanisms by which the brain of
a well fed but unloved child, to whom no one speaks and
with whom no one plays, deteriorates so completely that
the capacity to develop language can be lost forever. We
all know that children need playful interactions, challenges they can solve, caresses, smiles, lullabies, surprises,
joy . . . not only because it is a moral duty to give joy
to our little ones, but because if they don't get it, their
limbic brain stops developing and their capacity to relate
diminishes.

Scientists have studied the effect of love deprivation
on the brains of orphaned children for almost a century.
Bowlby's original 'attachment theory' has branched out
into the fields of neuropsychology, evolutionary psychology, and ethological theories. Attachment theories now
include the study of trauma and attachment patterns in
adults[18] and demonstrate how loss of love can turn into
a major trauma. Yet, with all this convincing research,
it seems that our culture ignores the fact that adults in
mourning need more than a week off from work *to get*

over it and *move on*. We should all take into consideration that grief can make us less capable than a trained rat in its familiar maze and that a week off is not enough. *All* individuals experiencing the loss of love report cognitive impairments: "I can't do the simplest work routine. I'll read a page of a report, and I barely understand what the sentences mean. I can't concentrate on the task. I keep making stupid mistakes. I can't think straight, my thoughts and emotions keep jumping like a crazy horse. I function at such a low level I dread going to work." Habitual neural circuits are deranged, and when the neuronal sluggishness lasts too long, there is synaptic degeneration. Love is the strongest life-sustaining factor; to see the person who provides it departing or dying is not only terrifying it is somatically dangerous, a major health risk. Heartbreak is a trauma, and like a PTSD, it brings past terrors in the present, it magnifies infantile traumas.[19]

Young mammals go from the initial phase of protest to the final stage of miasma in a consistent order. In human adults, the movement from the protest phase (the "don't be cruel" plea) to the final stage of somatic decline, can be interwoven. You go back and forth between protest and depression, depression and miasma, miasma and angry protest, alternating the crying in a darkened room, with jumpiness at the workplace. What is to be done with such misery?[20]

There you are my puppy!

Healing the heart after an emotional loss implies a rewiring of the mammalian brain responsible for emotional attachment. As opposed to reflexes, which cannot be modified, the limbic/emotional part of our brain is malleable and responds to *training*. Animal trainers use behavioral conditioning to produce a well-behaved dog, a compliant horse, and a competent working elephant. The emotional brain is where the phenomenon of mirror neurons has been observed. These are neurons that fire not only as we perform a certain action, but also when we watch someone else perform that same action: a mother watches her child in sheer rapture over licking an ice cream cone, and she, too, feels pleasure. We see somebody laughing his heart out, and we begin to laugh, even if we didn't get the joke. We observe the kitten jumping in the air to catch a butterfly, and we smile. Our dog greets us at the door, and his joyous excitement moves us. The discovery of this mechanism is key to the study of empathy and connectedness. It suggests that we are pre-wired for interacting and for wanting others around us. We share that capacity with other mammals—autism being the tragic exception.

The default response of our limbic brain is to fear abandonment because an abandoned newborn mammal inevitably dies; our brain never forgets that biological reality. Even if our adult self knows we are perfectly equipped to take care of our basic needs, there is still, in the folds of our brain, the memory of the earlier vulnerability. Anyone who has ever observed a lost puppy, kitten, colt, or calf, has seen the best demonstration of what psychologists call a co-dependent.

Co-dependence starts with a mammalian self, filled with puppy dreams of finding joy, safety, nurturance, support, fun, and play in a land of milk and honey, all free of charge. Your little puppy relational style is simple: "I'm cute, vulnerable and needy; it's your responsibility to take care of me". The honeymoon usually satisfies this infantile part in us, and we enjoy, for a time, the illusion that pleasure and security are here to stay. "My partner is wonderful: he or she takes care of all my needs." When suddenly the milk curdles and the honey stops flowing, because the partner betrays, dies, goes broke, works too much, loses interest, or finds a different fountain of love, the panic is intense, and it is a limbic panic. The memory of helplessness resurfaces and submerges the adult with an instinctual fear; it shows up *in every heartbroken individual, no exception.*

The psychiatric definition of Dependent /Codependent Personality Disorder is as follows: "A pervasive and excessive need to be taken care of which leads to submissive and clinging behavior and fears of separation, beginning by early adulthood and present in a variety of contexts, as indicated by five (or more) of the following:

1) Has difficulty making everyday decisions without an excessive amount of advice and reassurance from others.

2) Needs others to assume responsibility for most major areas of his or her life.

3) Has difficulty expressing disagreement with others because of fear of loss of support or approval.

4) Has difficulty initiating projects or doing things on his or her own, because of a lack of self-confidence in judgment or abilities rather than a lack of motivation or energy.

5) Goes to excessive lengths to obtain nurturance and support from others, to the point of volunteering to do things that are unpleasant.

6) Feels uncomfortable or helpless when alone because of exaggerated fears of being unable to care for himself or herself.

7) Urgently seeks another relationship as a source of care and support when a close relationship ends. 7) Is unrealistically preoccupied with fears of being left to take care of himself or herself."[21]

The DSM description is precise and I wish it were simply called the *portrait of an immature adult*, or the *portrait of a normal adult experiencing heartbreak*. Both are stuck at the stage of limbic attachment and fear, but the former is permanently handicapped while the latter can move out of the neurotic clinging. The DSM also fails to mention that this needy limbic self is *not only* a clinical problem; it is also at the core of the capacity to *bond* and to *receive*.

The limbic capacity to form attachment is at the core of all loving relationships, a place where we are allowed to feel our essential fragility and neediness. The limbic brain is where we feel sensual pleasure, playfulness and receptivity. The challenge for the adult personality is to keep the capacity to bond and receive, while lessening the infantile dependency.

The wolf separated from the pack: the broken heart syndrome

Hospital emergency rooms are filled with patients whose symptoms express a panic similar to that of the wolf separated from the pack, or that of a person shunned by the whole clan. It is a limbic panic. The panic that brings you to the hospital emergency room is called *stress cardiomyopathy*. Another name for it is *apical ballooning syndrome*, a condition of the heart that happens when the brain, following an emotional trauma, releases chemicals into the bloodstream that cause a swelling (ballooning) of the heart, and rapid and severe heart muscle weakness (*cardiomyopathy.*)[22] The symptoms are similar to patients having a heart attack and since heartbreak often provokes that reaction, it became known as the *broken heart syndrome*. The medical response to this syndrome is usually to administer a strong dose of Valium (diazepam).

Dr. Rich, the cardiologist from the Mayo clinic who educated the public about this syndrome, has this to say: *Apical ballooning syndrome (ABS) is a unique reversible cardiomyopathy that is frequently precipitated by a stressful event, and has a clinical presentation that is indistinguishable from a myocardial infarction. [...] The term Broken Heart Syndrome may not be the best name for this syndrome, as one typically thinks of a broken heart as something that occurs after receiving a Dear John letter, rather than something that happens after seeing a loaded .44 magnum shoved in one's face. Nonetheless, this terminology has resulted in lots of publicity, and the knowledge of this new syndrome consequently has been rapidly and widely disseminated. And that widespread awareness is good. The symptoms of BHS are so severe that it is nearly inconceivable that anyone who develops it will fail to seek medical help [...].*[23]

There is no medication that will make us wiser about love, but medication does sedate the mammalian panic;

that limited success has given Big Pharma the arguments to convince us that all psychic disorders are caused by "chemical imbalance" and that their magic bullets will cure it. Indeed, Valium is useful when experiencing the *broken heart syndrome,* yet medication can only take care of the crocodile and the puppy. It can never launch a chain of reactions to make us wiser, which is the only way out of the desert. Researchers are now looking at the tragic consequences for mental health when Big Pharma teams up with the DSM is medicating the brain instead of educating the whole person.[24]

When the partner is all, anchor and home base, security blanket and transcendent bliss, the experience of being abandoned by that most important person breaks our trust in all of humanity; we feel as if dropped by the mother, cursed by the father, snubbed by the sister, betrayed by the brother, delivered to the enemy by the friend. Of course the body carries heavy somatic consequences! Wasn't that obvious of all time?

The ego-shattering immensity of loss of love sends us into a spin of denial and reactivity. The experience of heartbreak is called *archetypal* because all humans, despite their talent, beauty, fame, intelligence, sooner or later experience helplessness and panic when love is denied. But no nurse, no medical doctor, no ER personnel will have that calming conversation with you. Medicating the panicky regressed person is what the medical profession is all about. If you know how limited is the effect of the sedative pill, you are already ahead of the curve. The mystery of love is one of the deepest aspect of the human heart; it is not up to your doctor to solve it. Know that, breathe deeply, and take your time, calm yourself: you are being initiated.

The art of consoling

Some environments, some friends, some therapists and some colleagues are such that they offer a consoling, calming presence. The word "consolation" is an old and poetic word that neuropsychologists would not want to be caught using; they like their jargon and prefer the concept of *limbic regulation*. A therapist who offers solace, reassurance and compassionate listening in a safe environment, has a consoling effect on the vulnerable self. Some individuals are more gifted than others in the art of consoling. It is a mysterious and beautiful ability, its value underestimated. In my own episode of heartbreak, a woman friend left on my pillow a nice soft flannel pajama, with a card that read, "Here is something for you to do your crying, in comfort!" Her gift, besides making me laugh, contained the mysterious power of consolation: I am not alone in this cold world, and this pajama is the proof. The opposite of consolation is competition: it sends the message that you better get over it as fast as you can: "this is the Hunger Games, no time for mourning, get back in the arena."

The young pup that resides in our limbic brain needs not only compassionate others but also some reassurance that pleasure is still possible. Anything that activates the pleasure principle, laughter, a massage, a good meal, even masturbation[25] can be considered "limbic regulation". Just like a hug and an ice cream cone can console a crying child, it is crucial for you to find sources of pleasure that don't involve the partner.

A study on bonding and befriending among women revealed how women cope with stress in the workplace by getting together to chat and talk about the situation. Drs. Klein and Taylor at UCLA[26] discovered that men typically isolate themselves in their office while women get together, which releases oxytocin—the hormone of bonding between mother and baby. Men also produce this substance, but not when testosterone dominates their reaction.

This study confirms previous studies that show how supportive social ties reduce our risk of disease by lowering blood pressure, heart rate, and cholesterol. Often, the therapist's office is the only place were support is offered. Many researchers have tried to understand what exactly is transformative when you talk with your therapist. Cambray and Carter (2004) for example, examine how a depth psychological approach will facilitate what they call an *emergent process* in which the psyche self-organizes along a vertical axis toward individuation. In simpler words, the trajectory from trauma to psychological health is possible only if both therapist and patient are interacting at the deepest and most embodied, honest, and generous level of their psyche. A previous generation of psychoanalysts call this *transference and countertransference*, but, however you call it, bonding is a phenomenon that takes place in all human relations, at various levels.

There are degrees of intensity between the consoling effect of a soft pajama given by a friend, and the radical transforming of one's psyche that is the result of years of analysis. Nevertheless, when the limbic brain is in distress, one should not look down at the benefits of good company.

This being said, the consoling strategy has it limits because we are not only vulnerable puppies and babies. The fact that children make and need attachment objects has unfortunately been used in popular psychology as a blueprint for adult relations. As Adam Philips writes: "In psychoanalytic stories it is as though the adult is always succumbing to the child within. But it is one of the advantages of growing up that one can extend the repertoire of possible relationships."[27]

Neuromania and Darwinitis

To benefit from neuroscience you don't need to become a "neuromaniac". Philosopher Raymond Tallis defines *neuromania* as a tendency to reduce human consciousness (and love) to the firing of neurons. Like Tallis, I am Darwinian, in the sense that I believe in evolution, but objects to neuroscience's biologism, which is a reduction of the mind to the brain. If it is all in the brain, our justice system ceases to make sense because ultimately one could always argue: "my brain chemistry was unbalanced and I could not control my anger". For the same reasons, he deconstructs what he calls *darwinitis*, a refusal to acknowledge the crucial difference between humans and animals. Tallis writes: "A chimpanzee reaches out or begs for a banana and consumes it. Darwinitics calls it "feeding behavior" and puts it in the same category as you and I going to the restaurant."

I, for one, never met a chimp who knows the difference between the fish fork, the dinner fork, the salad fork, the butter plate, the service plate, the red wine glass, the white wine glass, the champagne glass. No chimp, however smart has ever written a cookbook, plan a dinner party on Doodle, spent money on a lace tablecloth, put candles and flowers on the table as part of his "feeding behavior."[28] Neuroscientists use the word "joy" for a rat enjoying chocolate, but no rat has ever produced an equivalent of the *Ode to Joy*, which is movement four in Beethoven's ninth symphony. Biologism ignores the human capacity for wisdom and love, our most glorious achievement.

Is it in my genes, my brain or my soul?

Psychological models come and go. The defunct myth of modernity suggested: *my body is a machine,* and doctors with by their surgical and pharmaceutical toolkit can repair it if it breaks. This early mechanistic view of the body was replaced by genomics, with its new myth: *it's all in my genes,* until this view too was debunked by geneticists themselves. The cover of *Life in* 2010 posted: *You are not your genes.* The dominance of genetics was immediately followed by the dominance of neuroscience: *it is all in my brain,* until geneticists debunked their own myth and concluded *we are not our brains.* The actual consensus in neuroscience is now that we are the result of the connection between *brain and culture.* Here the word *culture* means *everything* in our environment, including all that is an expression of the right brain capability to imagine, symbolize, put in music, express through art, literature, political ideologies, religion... in a word, everything that lives in that big bag of ideas and productions called *culture.*

As Hofstadter wrote: *"An "I " is a strange loop in a brain where symbolic and physical levels feed back into each other and flip causality upside down, with symbols seeming to have gained the paradoxical ability to push particles around, rather than the reverse*".[29] This connection between brain and culture is the basis of all forms of education, from good manners to the highest achievements in the humanities. It is also the surest road to take if one wants to recover from heartbreak. More than medication to sedate the croc and lessen the anxiety of the pup, the heartbroken individual needs to move beyond those levels and "push the particles around".

Becoming a wise human

A child can attract the attention of the parent with an injury: "look Ma, I'm bleeding." A codependent adult makes the mistakes of using this infantile strategy (*I need you because I hurt*) long after it is acceptable. It may attract pity, but not love. The wise human is someone capable of evolving beyond the crocodilian reactivity and beyond the limbic terrors of being abandoned. It is not so much the pitiful codependent in us that is problematic—it is there in all of us, from the beginning—but rather the lack of development of the wise human.

Telling your story of heartbreak to friends, family and therapist can indeed be consoling; it is even necessary, but only up to a point, because healing heartbreak is not the re-establishment of a limbic sense of secure attachment. The only way to reach beyond this point is to move into the higher functions of our human brain, as opposed to the mammalian self.

What Jung called the process of individuation, and philosophers called the quest for wisdom, is what ultimately makes the difference between those who learn something from their heartbreak and those who remain lost in the desert of neurotic patterns of attachment. What is the use of *creativity* if not to elevate our limbic meowing, growling, and howling to the level of the eternal human drama?

As a psychologist, one of the things that still amaze me is the fact that we can *educate* our emotions to become wiser about love and relationships. I find it sad that there is no training of emotions offered in schools. I would like to see *Love 101*, *Anger 101,* and *Fear 101* starting in kindergarten!

The process of getting an education is *simple*, yet, it is not *simplistic*. The kind of self-help industry that focuses exclusively on the positive is an incompetent teacher because to become a good driver, one has to be taught how driving a car can kill you, kill others, and send you to prison. The positive is obvious but the negative is not. The car is both one of the most dangerous objects in our cultural environment, *and* an object that can augment our freedom. Learning to drive is simple, yet there is a learning curve, as well as an emotional and even moral dimension to it. The same is true when it comes to educating our emotions, especially around love, which triggers jealousy, possessiveness, and fear. Simplicity is beautiful; simplification is catastrophic. Positive thinking is a lovely idea, but as Ehrenreich's (2009) recent research has shown, the relentless promotion of positive thinking has negative side effects; it fails to boost self-esteem and instead augments narcissism, self-indulgence and incompetence. Educating our emotions includes developing a healthy sense of the difficulties in any relationships and the capacity to see one's shadow. To receive an education, we imitate someone who knows more than we do. We examine our errors, not only our successes; we practice and observe the fine points; we read, discuss, think, talk, try to solve ever more complex problems. We do it for as long as it takes to become as good as the master; and then, if we have it in us, we surpass the teacher. A master is anybody who is competent at something you want to learn, and capable of communicating precise feedback of your performance.

When Jung was formulating his theory of individuation, he was influenced by the Indian yogic system of lower and higher chakras. Living from one's lower chakras exemplifies the concept of living from one's animal nature (the crocodile and the puppy). Mammals do have a cerebral cortex, variable in size; for example, the cortex of a rabbit is pitifully small compared to that of a dog, which is why no magician was ever able to teach a rabbit to curtsy as it comes out of the hat.

The process of individuation is certainly not a denial of the lower chakras, but an affirmation of the highest possible form of wisdom reserved for humans. The human cortex is proportionally twice as big as that of any other mammal, and with abilities that are unique. As our neocortical neural structure evolved, we developed not only the capacity for sophisticated language, art, science, music, but also a capacity to love at the deep level that we do. Humans yearn for the fullest possible experience of love, which can exist only at the highest level of our evolution. Puppy love and the symbiotic attachment of mother and child are foundational, beautiful, necessary, likewise, the bond with our pet animal, can be gratifying and cozy, but this kind of bonding is not the full expression of the human capacity to love, nor is the disturbance of the limbic regulation the full expression of the catastrophe of human heartbreak.

The inner and the outer

Love provokes an *inner* expansion that augments the capacity to feel the beauty of the *outer* world. Lovers have memories of admiring a starry sky as if they had never seen the sky before; of tasting food as if the number of taste buds had suddenly multiplied; of making love and hitting seventh heaven. Love, an inner experience, unites inner and outer because perception of the outer world is neurologically connected to the inner psychic experience: expansion of inner realm provokes a multiplication of the neurons that allow us to experience the outer world. In other words, the larger the inner landscape, the larger one sees of the outer.

In the euphoric period of falling in love, this expansion is easy and pleasurable; like a toddler learning language at an astonishing speed, lovers learn fast and adopt new behaviors that solidify their bond. Change is easy and adaptation is fast; falling in love means our learning capacities are exercised at their maximum. It is also the case with any important new experience -- new job, new country, new challenge. When in Rome, we learn to do like the Romans; when in love we learn to do what serves the relationship.

The loss of the beloved brings the reverse experience: an incapacity and a refusal to adjust to the new situation. The heart is still wide open and the neurons are firing, but that openness is now felt as painful, because the connection to the beloved is broken. Your vulnerable heart won't stop feeling, won't close; it remains painfully open because the neurons that connected you to your partner are firing in a void. You can't help wanting the partner to come back and literally reconnect you to the world, to yourself, and to each other. It is a triple disconnect.

At the time when love was plentiful, even mundane tasks had an amplified meaning; cooking, fixing things in the house, choosing the new color to repaint the walls, mixing cement to build a little fountain in the garden, teaching the child to use the digital camera to send grandpa an email . . . it all made sense because it expressed all that is meant by the words home, family, and love. Love reveals what a philosopher might call the *transcendent quality* of human life. Love brings an accentuation of our being, like a number squared; it is the revelation of something beyond the evidence of the senses.

Love grounds us in the concreteness of daily life, in our bodies, in our houses, in nature; it reflects the infinity of the cosmos in the inner sanctum of the heart. When the loving connection is broken, the lack of echo with the world is an inner abyss into which one falls. The bitterness of mourning has *the same amplifying power* as had the sweetness of love, but in reverse. The daily routine that felt so meaningful now feels painful, because it reveals a loss that feels like a cosmic loss.

We readily admit that both the bitter and the sweet are part of the love potion, but until we are forced to drink it to the dregs, we rarely take the time to analyze the bitterness lying in the bottom of the cup. Yet, this substance is needed to open the gates to the unconscious, to see what lies in the pre-verbal, implicit memory.

The Buddhists notion of adulthood includes the ability to take a position in the psyche that they personify as "the Witness". It is a psychic posture that allows the wise adult to observe the flow of what is, without the ego intervening to manipulate it. "Here is my crocodile, ready to bite, and here comes my puppy, needy, teary, clingy. I see you both, I feel your reactivity. Let it be!" The Witness simply observes the stream of events, without acting out. The Witness is present to both the inner and the outer, the mind and the body. The Witness does not identify with either pole. The Witness has the *detached presence* of consciousness.

The state of witnessing is a foundation on which you can rest your heart; it is the mindfulness that put you on the road to freedom of the heart.

The next chapter examines different meaning of the notion of the unconscious, and the necessity of a plunge in it to recover from heartbreak.

Chapter 2

Neuroscience and the importance of the unconscious

Staying with the darkness allows something to happen that escapes us if we are hasty. If we resist our natural tendency to take flight before painful experiences, we can descend into the dark aspects of the unconscious, which is necessary if we are to make contact with what Goethe calls infinite nature. Turning toward such darkness requires a willingness to stay with suffering and to make a descent into the unconscious. Stanton Marlan [30]

No one should deny the danger of the descent, but it can be risked. No one need risk it, but it is certain that some will. And let those who go down the sunset way do so with open eyes, for it is a sacrifice which daunts even the gods. Yet every descent is followed by an ascent; the vanishing shapes are shaped anew, and the truth is valid in the end only if it suffers change and bears new witness in new images, in new tongues, like a wine that is put into new bottles.
Carl Jung[31]

I have a friend, a weather journalist, who likes to tell his story in the words of neuroscience because he does not know any of the vocabulary of depth psychology. He loves to read about neuroscience in popular science magazines and his understanding of himself is the best example I could find of how neuroscience redefines the psychoanalytic concept of the unconscious.

My life in a copter

I come from a family of mountain dwellers. The older members of my family are all familiar with the sound of a coming avalanche, a sound that provokes in all of them an instinctual state of alarm. The sound of avalanche is a trigger of the instinctual flight reaction; it means "here is an enemy too big to fight, it is better to flee!" Luckily, we have other options besides running out of the house like a bunch of horses caught in fire. Our rational judgment kicks in and when roads are not safe, somebody calls the rescue helicopter.

I was one year old when I experienced my first avalanche. Soon after, my parents divorced and I left the Alps with my mother, to live in Canada. The sound of an avalanche is one I heard in my mother's arms, when she was in a state of utter panic. Everybody around her, all of them as panicky as she was, got together outside the house, to wait for the rescue helicopter.

Two neuronal associations were created in my brain: the first one is a pre-verbal sensory memory that says here is a sound (avalanche) and a smell (the smell of snow) that means danger. The second association says: here is another sound (the copter motor) that means safety and you can trust that sound.

I was unaware that such a bundle of synapses had re-mained in my brain. I was told the story of that ava-lanche at fifty. Until then I never knew what had mo-tivated my choice of becoming a weather journalist. You see, I spend all my working hours in a helicopter and I detest the smell of snow, which is why I came to live in California.

My friend has a neurologically correct story: a child's limbic capacity is developed enough to register mom and dad's panic, but until eighteen months, because language is not yet developed, the child cannot interpret the *context* (i.e. the full story going on around him.) A child is a limbic genius when it comes to *feeling* the panic signals or the soothing signals coming from the adults. When the rescue helicopter came in, although its motor made a much louder noise than the avalanche, my friend's infan-tile brain learned the following lesson: trust mom, who trusts the rescuers, who trust the copter, but don't ever trust the sound of an avalanche, nor the smell of snow.

Any incident that happens before the hippocampus (part of the limbic brain) is fully developed makes the stocking of *explicit memory*[32] impossible and is respon-sible for *infantile amnesia*. Nevertheless, the experience leaves a trace in the brain called an *implicit memory,* a notion very similar to that of the unconscious. As language develops, the child starts being able to remember a context and a time sequence, because the *words* to tell the story are available. The retrieval of such memory is sometimes called *episodic memory*, or *autonoetic memory* (i.e. knowing that I know). Some authors also refer to it as *narrative memory* to point to the fact that it is a form of memory that includes a time sequence. For example, if you tell the factual details of a car accident, you will remember that it took place last week, mid-morning, there was a sedan on the left . . . a red truck coming from the right . . . rain and fog . . . a frontal impact. You organize the events in a time sequence, a *story* of the accident, with its episodes and narrative style.

Neuroscientists point out an interesting detail: the act of recollecting and reflecting upon one's past is neurologically similar to the act of *anticipating* one's future. Although we never use the word *memory* when imagining our future, but rather words like imagination, day dreaming, planning, fantasizing, yet it is fascinating to learn that it is a neurologically similar operation to reminiscing.[33] By contrast to the *autonoetic* (I know that I know) memory, with which we know we are in the act of recollecting a story, the *noetic* (knowing) memory is one where we don't need to recall the past to remember something that has become a semiconscious routine, like reaching for your car keys in your purse or driving your car from work to home.

My friend was not told the story of the avalanche until he was fifty years old. The fact that the smell of snow triggered an automatic reaction of unease had remained an unexplained mystery. He never could understand his physical nervousness whenever he visited his father's family in the Alps in winter. He never knew why he had so wanted to become a weather reporter, *spending all his working hours in a helicopter*; and he never explored what motivated his choice to live in California, where there are no snowfalls. When told of the avalanche episode, a new awareness was possible and he could distinctively *feel* his fear of the smell of snow and his fear of any sound resembling the low growling of avalanche.

This example does not suggest that the unconscious is an anatomical structure, nor does it suggest that the story told to Bill about the avalanche is the absolute truth; maybe he was uncomfortable in the Alps because he is uncomfortable around the paternal side of his family! Nevertheless, it raises questions about his somatic aversion to snow and his attraction for helicopters. Depth psychologists call this an unconscious reaction, while neuroscientists call it *implicit memory*, or *a memory without a context*[34]. However you name it, it remains the key to understanding what triggers maladjusted reactions.

Heartbreak is an experience where the preverbal fear of abandonment comes back in full force and rings an alarm in the brain. Just like the discomfort around snow says: "Alert! An avalanche is coming", heartbreak says: "alert! "Loss of love coming." The brain remembers that for the little mammal, loss of love is a lethal risk. You can try to convince your rational brain that abandonment does not run the same risk as in the past but it won't register until the pre-verbal panic is made conscious. There is a subroutine on the hard disk of our memory that generates panic at loss of love. This fear-generating automatic alarm system is a standard attachment to all human psyches; the only way to bypass it is to examine the fear *consciously*, to observe it as if from the outside. Examine your fear like you would examine a skin rash.

The end of the behaviorists's dominance

In the past fifty years, the goal of behavioral-cognitive approaches has consistently been to bypass the notion of the unconscious. Behavioral-cognitive theorists critiqued depth psychology relentlessly, suggesting it is a waste of time to look into the unconscious because if you change the cognition (i.e. the conscious beliefs and ideas), the behavior will change accordingly, so why bother with the unconscious? For sure, cognition and the training of behavior is the basis of all pedagogy; in a sense, every parent is a bevaviorist practitioner: "eat your brocoli if you want dessert". And every parent is a cognitivist: "do you get the idea honey?"

Yet, in denying the usefulness of the notion of the unconscious, cognitive-behavioral approaches refused to take into account the hidden *feeling* behind the thinking and the doing. They snubbed depth psychologists for their interest in symbols, metaphors, myths, as if all that were a costly unnecessary detour that only the bourgeois elite can afford.

In short, the cognitive/behavioral approaches ignored half the brain! They did not want to hear that defense mechanisms, or anything in the psyche, may have unconscious roots. The game changer is the confirmation by neuroscience that some connections in the psyche are active even without our conscious knowing. Even more annoying if you are a bev-cog fundamentalist, neuroscience demonstrate how a *symbolic reconfiguration* (the subject of Volume One) must accompany the cognitive effort if we are to get deep enough change to affect the whole personality. Behavioral psychologists refused to use concepts such as defense mechanism, repressed contents, or dissociative states.

Some psychologist, such as Allan Schore[35] differentiates *repression* from *dissociation*; the former implies a content that would have to be conscious before it is repressed, while the latter does not enter consciousness because it is too threatening. Both repression and dissociation are defense mechanisms that become neurotic patterns as we keep responding to the present with attitudes and behaviors that are from the past. To stop the waste of psychic energy, one has to keep the heart open, tolerate the heat, and let the fear emerge to consciousness. If you can do that, your wise inner adult will show up. Your inner images will translate into action, and action into fresh images.

You can't repair the past

I knew a woman whom everyone thought of as the ultimate image of success: bright, sexy, mature, charming, competent, a warm and decent woman whom everyone admired and loved. She fell in love with a narcissistic and shallow man, who betrayed her regularly and almost absentmindedly. Her friends saw the obvious: this boyfriend was a copy of her narcissistic father and she was trying to get from him the attention she never received from the father. But she was not conscious of her unresolved father complex.

Later, I had a similar, but reversed surprise with a former student who, at twenty-seven, was considered by his classmates as an immature, self-centered playboy, the kind of man who boasted of having used every woman who ever approached him. One day he expressed his love and admiration to an older woman, a friend of his family, and found himself politely dismissed. After a few unsuccessful attempts to establish a romantic connection with her, he went home and committed suicide, leaving behind a love letter to her. We were all stunned! He had a heart after all? His was obviously a neurotic infatuation, because he barely knew this woman, but heartbreak based on an illusion of love is not necessarily easier to get over than heartbreak based on *true love*. In both cases, that of the brilliant woman betrayed by an immature partner, and that of the egoistic student rejected by a woman he barely knew, *something* in the rejection was insufferable; somehow it felt easier to commit suicide than to go through the pain of examining the past wound. Both of them were trying to repair the past.

We confuse the eternal archetype of love with the person who inspires it, because our brain analyzes the present with the lessons from the past. The caregivers were our first divinities (or our first abusers). The positive feeling we had towards them is later transferred to the person of the partner, and he or she appears with the halo of the original divinity. "Ah! It is You, Sweet Lover. I remember how it felt to have my every need met; come fill my heart, I've missed you". When the partner suddenly fails to deliver the honey, the shock is intense: "How dare you drop me so cruelly! I need you so completely"

The brain not only confuses the lover with the unconscious mother complex, but also often creates a split between the Good Mother and the Terrible Mother. If the biological mother was lacking, the projection on the partner feels as if, at last, we have found paradise. "Your love feels safer, more generous, more joyous than what I got from my mother; you are what I craved and never got." As long as the partner gives us the honey of unconditional love, which is the positive side of the mother archetype, we are in the honeymooner's paradise. When that idealized transference is shattered, we find ourselves in hell.

There is a kind of logic in every feeling, a *psycho-logic* and there is logic, too, in our expectation that love should repair past wounding, because every deep, loving relationship has the power to heal. "My mother thought I was ugly, but you say I am beautiful and my heart believes you. Oh Joy!" Yet, there is one essential condition for love to work its healing magic: *the original wounding first has to be made conscious, in order to accept that the past cannot be repaired.* Otherwise, one stays forever in the idealized transference, an illusion that must be shattered for the psyche to mature.

The awareness of the original wounding was made possible for William, the case we examined in detail in Volume One, when he *recognized,* in his begging for Laura's affection, the very same lack he experienced with his mother. Laura's rejection felt exactly the same as his mother's aloofness. "Eureka! I get it, I am reacting to the past, when I could not walk away."

Without an awareness of our parental complexes, the need to repair inevitably becomes too much of a burden for the partner, and the relationship is bound to break down. The partner cannot help feeling: "I am not the one who broke your spirit, cut your wings, said you were ugly, stupid, and a loser; why should I atone, expiate, repair, compensate for damage I did not cause? You are not with me in *our* story, you are engaged with the villains of your past" Such a relationship is insulated from the reality of the present, and it becomes too rigid to survive.

Any relationship, including friendship, which is in "repair mode" most of the time *has* to break down. The individual who remains unconscious of the past wounding is basically saying: "give me more, give me always, fix me, help me, because I did not receive enough in the past." We all have had the experience of crossing out somebody from our list of friends because there is never any possibility of reciprocity. The breakdown of those relationships is a response from nature that delivers a crucial truth in order to evolve: the past, because it is past, can never be fixed!

However, a wounding from the past *can* be transformed into something that enhances emotional intelligence, once we accept that although the past itself cannot be changed, we can change our actual mode of relating to it. Heartbreak is saying: "When will you understand that you will *never* have the loving, competent, warm-hearted, nurturing mother you so needed as a child? Do I have to be Mother Earth because you did not get enough of that milk of compassion?" Or it is saying: "When will you get over the fact that your daddy was, and will remain for all eternity, a lousy alcoholic bum incapable of supporting his family? Why should I provide for all your needs because he didn't?"

It is a sad thing to see a woman complaining of not finding the partner who would take care of her *the way she would like!* She is in *repair mode* and wants to *have had* a generous, competent dad. Since it is a desire to change the past, it can never be satisfied in the present. If a partner shows up, willing to try, it is never enough, and confirms the woman's belief that all men are abandoners, just like daddy. Her *idea* of love is such that no living soul can ever compete with the fantasy.

Again, there is logic to the psyche: no amount of loving by an actual person can ever fill the abysmal pit of cravings that comes from a past trauma, if that trauma remains unconscious. It is the *unconsciousness of the trauma, not the trauma itself* that creates the unrealistic expectations, the repeated failures, and the chronic disappointment. It leads to the loveless isolation that the person is complaining about.

The only remedy is to look at our disappointments and heartbreaks as a call from nature, a psychic alarm saying:

it is now time to evolve beyond your immature dream of being saved, healed, taken care of (financially, emotionally, socially, intellectually, physically.) All adolescents daydream about the divine lover, the one who will give them identity and security, motherlove and motherland, fatherlove and fatherland, money and honey, but it is a terrible handicap when such dreams persist in the adult personality.

In a culture where the dominant values are around money, fame, sex and power, the unconscious expectations often translate in those same terms; yet even an abundance of money, fame or sex will fail to deliver healing for a lack that has remained unconscious. The potential for evolution is immense: heartbreak can shatter for good the dream of a symbiotic paradise and force an end to the idealized projections.

The slave complex

If only our carrying our loved one's pain took the burden off their shoulders, it might be the generous thing to do. Unfortunately, when our sacrifice comes from a neurotic self-denial, it does more harm than good. Veronica comes from a family in which love is interpreted as reciprocal enslavement, as if there were a silent injunction that says: "nobody in this house should outgrow their limitations."

Veronica never imagined an identity for herself, apart from the one given by her family. I saw her after a suicide attempt.

No ego, no Self, no identity.

I don't have a definition of myself. Like my mother and grandmother, I always chose the piece of meat that was overcooked, leaving the best for the others, although I was the one cooking all those gourmet meals; I tolerated my kids talking on their cell phones while eating my gourmet dinners, treating me like a waitress.

I was the kind of woman who jumped up to do the dishes while still chewing on my last bite of food, hopping on the next task. I believed that a husband's sexual attitude of Wham, Bam, Thank you Ma'am was natural.

Veronica's third divorce was the first time she really let herself *feel* her alienation. She had to deconstruct, demolish, re-format her psychic hard disk to install a new identity. It is a difficult task, one that does not happen until the old identity is utterly broken. Being abandoned for the third time was the occasion.

My fundamental attitude was always to save the day! I had no revolt as if I had been born to please. The slave complex! I thought I was the perfect victim until I looked beneath and found the huge power trip behind my victim's posturing.

Serving their needs gave me control. I wanted control, as opposed to love, because I was at the lowest rung of human achievement: survival. I didn't have a self, how could I have a sensual self? I never felt love, not even for my children, and never saw the beauty in the world. I just survived. Either I become a real person, or I will kill that empty shell that is me.

Veronica's heartbreak was a form of guidance from nature: "you are hurting now, but you'll die if you pursue your old ways." The guidance is extreme, but so is nature: swim or sink, fly or crash, leave this milieu, those values, this belief, this group, this job, this Church, this city, this program, this clique, this partner . . . or you'll lose your vitality! Nature has no patience for those who can't adapt. The process of heartbreak-through is a frenzy of destruction for an identity that fails to support the evolutionary process. Traumatic learning is still learning, and each time our emotional life moves into the chaos of heartbreak, it is an occasion to let go of outmoded, damaging forms of attachment.

Even when it came to feel more *natural* to live in the confined space of your fearful heart, still there is always the option to deconstruct and reconstruct. Be prepared to experience a new, more interesting form of fear, the fear of adventure. On the day they are freed, long time prisoners are often afraid to leave their prison; the world seems too vast, and the discovery of its beauty brings an acute misery at the thought of the wasted years, the lost life. Veronica had made herself comfortable in her domestic prison, and the intuition of all the wasted joy, the friendships avoided, the life unlived, the occasions wasted, provoked an intense fear that at first paralyzed her.

Nevertheless, with the shock of a third divorce, and thanks to a period of forced solitude as well as some therapeutic help, she started rebuilding a sense of Self along a different set of values. Her fear gave way to excitement, and she began scrubbing clean the gluey neurotic attachment to an outdated, sacrificial, self-denying identity.

I am garbage!

I was married for twenty-five years. I was wife, mistress, secretary, big and little sister, confidante, confessor, guru, cook, janitor, accountant. I was his baby, his mommy, his queen, his whore, and his Madonna.

With the end of our marriage, all my titles are gone. I am free to become whomever I wish, but I have no idea who that person should be, what she could do, or where she should live, how, and for what purpose.

I used to love reading, but I can't read; I don't know what I want to read. I used to be an active person, and now I stay in my pajamas all day, eating whatever I find in the kitchen that is still edible.

Veronica is in the process of letting go of an identity that *has to be left behind;* yet, in that transition, she is naked in the cold! Her therapy is a process of slowly discovering the person she can and wants to be. That process is one of *initiation* because the change is not a simple transition from one set of activities to another. It is a profound transformation of all aspects of the personality.

At the core of any initiation, there is a letting go of the previous identity, the typical ritual requiring that the neophyte remain *in solitude*, forced to face the angst. As elements of the previous identity are stripped away, the elders, or teachers, or guides do not explain to the neophyte the details of the initiation process. Lost are the usual objects, places, modes of relating, in order to send the neophyte a very clear message: "Your past identity is gone, a new one is coming; but in between, you have to remain alone with the terror of the void."

That fear has its utility: it pushes the neophyte into the next stage of life, want it or not, because the community blocks the way back so that there is no other way but forward. When the initiate is ready to be reinstated in the community, the new identity that emerges has more vitality than the one that was shed. The initiation was successful.

A heartbreak-through follows the same process: the way back is blocked, and you have no choice but to go through periods of angst, alienation, isolation, fear of the void, tears. Although the deconstruction is painful, it offers a rare occasion to update your connectors. Slowly, you should start changing little things: your wardrobe, or your computer, or your décor, or your reading habits, or your routines, or your friends, as long as it answers the question: "is this something that my new self might like?"

Veronica spent her childhood trying to support her frustrated unhappy mother, to rescue her abused grandmother, to assist her sick and overworked father, to make ends meet, and to survive on a farm with little comfort and little money. It hurts to see a parent suffer, so she carried the pain of her mother and became *mother bound*; she carried the pain of her father and became *father bound.*

Not only did Veronica grow up to be blind to her own lack of self, she also lived with an inner injunction that communicated: "Thou shall not evolve past the point reached by your ancestors; don't you dare be happier (sexier, richer, more educated) than the people from your clan." Later, as an adult, she offered her "services" instead of her love, because this is how she had learned to relate.

I have inherited the frigidity of a whole lineage of heroic women, all of whom survived by denying their material, emotional, sexual and spiritual needs. Like my female forebears, I offered my husbands sexual service, domestic service, secretarial service, catering service . . . never risking to exist for my sake.

My first husband left me for a woman I find vulgar and ugly, but, according to him, one who likes sex. He left me with four kids to raise, which, of course, I did heroically. When the youngest left for college, I met my second husband, and I thought it would be different.

But soon I was back to the same game of doing whatever he wanted. He wanted to have another child, to insure that he and I would be a "real" family, thus making it quite clear that my other four kids, because they were not biologically his, did not qualify as real family.

I did not oppose that silly egocentrism of his, and I gave birth to a fifth child, which I didn't really want. I think he wanted that child to tie me more securely to the hitching post of marriage and domestic responsibility. Our baby girl was his puppy. As soon as she was old enough to argue with him, he lost interest in her, and he himself became my needy baby.

CHAPTER 3

WHAT YOU MOTHER NEVER TOLD YOU

Your partner is not your parent, which means that if you are still infantile, you must finish growing up on your own. If you have had a multitude of breakups, maybe it is time for an honest examination of your destructive attitudes. Passive-aggressive behaviors are among the most crazy-making, the most widespread, and the most destructive of relationships.

From time to time, we all need to take an honest inventory of the ways in which we drive our partners away. In psychiatric terms, passive-aggressive behavior is not in the same category as other severe clinical syndromes; it is rather like a general failure to grow up and take responsibility for one's need. It is characterized by a habitual pattern of *passive resistance to expectations* from co-workers, partners, friends and family. Resistance is exhibited by such indirect behaviors as procrastination, forgetfulness, and purposeful inefficiency, in reaction to demands by authority figures, parents, or partners.

I am a champion procrastinator

My partner asks that I pay half the rent, half the groceries and do my share around the house. I like to appear rational, sweet, competent and lovable, so I say "yes, certainly". But I procrastinate, I give half of what I owe, I invent excuses, I lie. The partner becomes confused, angry: "where is the money?" I pout, sulk, and complain: "why do you expect so much of me? Don't you love me?" I procrastinate on everything and with everybody: my partner, my parents, my colleagues, my friends; I procrastinate with doing the tax return, paying the bills, doing the laundry, washing the dishes, answering an email, writing a report, updating the website, visiting my parents, making an appointment, buying the plane tickets for our vacation, everything! I say I'll do it and then I make the other wait and wait and wait. I can drag my feet to appear as if the task is monumental, although it really isn't. The partner gets

wary of waiting, and expresses frustration, anger, which makes him/her the bad one! I shake my head and sigh, or fake a handicap, or walk away in tears. I follow up with the silent treatment, a most efficient punishment for anybody who dare have expectations.

A passive-aggressive personality is another name for an immature adult. It is anybody who, under normal circumstances, expects the partner to take more than his/her half of responsibilities.

I am dependent but won't admit it

I have difficulty being alone, I don't like my own company, I fear rejection, I won't do the things I should be doing to become financially, emotionally, professionally independent. I waste my talents on silly activities, I obsess about the wrong things, I lack ambition, I won't control my expenses, I create drama. I don't take responsibility for my needs, my duties, my failures. I don't like to say thank you. I am as dependent as a teenager who wants freedom but won't pay the bills. I use every method of control to avoid the partner leaving me; inducing guilt is a favorite: "how terrible you are for not taking care of poor little me."

Like a child, a passive-aggressive adult tries to get away with incompetence. He/she won't admit responsibility for a mistake. For fear of being found out, the passive aggressive individual will put up with shows of superiority, or will express disdain for the standards of performance ("the problem is not me, it's micro-management!")

I feel inadequate but cover it with uppityness

I am not proud of myself. I have talents but waste them. I fear competition, I don't prepare well when there is a test, I expect perfection from others but won't admit my mistakes.

I have a collection of excuses, stories, and lies, such as: "Sorry I am late, it is the traffic" (again); "Sorry I did not get your message, my message box is full" (as usual); "I cannot talk for long, my phone battery is low" (again); "I can't confirm my schedule for now (stay on hold).

To confuse the partner and avoid responsibility, and appear as the victim, the passive-aggressive person will avoid giving a straight answer and will remain unclear about his/her my plan or intention. Mixed messages not only confuse the other, it allows the classic excuse: "you misunderstood what I said (silly you!)"

Passive-aggressive behaviors are like weeds. A few weeds in a garden are not a problem, but there is a point where it kills the garden. Any partner with a healthy sense of self can smell a passive-aggressive personality, like one smells fire. The good news is that those weeds can be eradicated.

YOUR SECOND CHANCE AT GROWING UP

> *Real love is wild and sad; a*
> *palpitating duo in the dark.*
> *Bachelard*[36]

The principles of evolution and of maturation recapitulate many of the most fascinating discoveries of neuroscience, among which are the demonstration of how your brain can help you grow up, or keep you infantile. Your brain:

a) reacts to the quality of your milieu,

b) is influenced by the level and quality of your intellectual activity,

c) responds to the atmosphere of interpersonal exchanges,

d) is hungry for new learning,

e) can evolve quickly, when facing adversity, leaping forward in a surprising evolutionary jump,

f) or can regress and degenerate as quickly, when deprived of stimulation.

Neuroscientists are telling you, in a nutshell, that depending on the milieu and on your willingness to take action, your brain either evolves or regresses, what some call the *use it or lose it theory*.[37] If you live in a rigid cultural milieu, closed to new ideas, with little opportunity for new friends, new world views, and new challenges, your brain adjusts by a minimal development of neuronal connections which means that you'll regress in a state of passive waiting for rescue. You may wait for the next magical lover to replace the lost one, and you may imagine redemption as something coming from *outside*.

If, on the other hand, you take action, the learning centers of your brain will follow that impetus. What the French psychiatrist Boris Cyrulnick[38] calls a *marvelous misfortune* is one that forces adaptation; the brain understand that something has to be done, quick, and it gets busy. Heartbreak is such a *marvelous misfortune*; it has the potential to change your personality. Nobody should waste the occasion.

Contrary to the Darwinian theory of slow evolution, it is now accepted that the brain's capacity to adapt can be much quicker than was formerly imagined. If the environment offers options, the brain is capable of quantum leaps.[39] The enduring controversy of nature versus nurture, biology versus culture, seems to have come to rest with the admission of the equality of both the nature and nurture principles, at least when mammals are concerned. Jaak Panksepp summarizes the consensus: "Thus, while basic emotional circuits are among the tools provided by *nature*, their ability to permanently change the life course and personalities of organisms depends on the *nurturance,* or lack of nurturance, that the world provides."[40]

Neuroscience has also established the fact that we think, feel, imagine with our *whole body,* the croc, the pup and the wise human working as a team. We think, perceive, feel, imagine, analyze with the whole brain, never with one side only. The distinction between right and left brain is not an either/or kind of opposition, but rather a question of balance and focus. Not only do we use all four sides of the brain simultaneously, we also think and feel either *in unison,* or *in conflict* with the world surrounding us. Both the unison and the conflict are formative. The nature/nurture controversy is as passé as the Cartesian dichotomy of mind-body.

The relationship between environment and brain is a feedback loop: the brain is shaped by culture, and the community of brains shapes culture. The hordes of heartbroken individuals who live the rest of their lives with a scarred and scared heart are those who remain isolated in an outdated myth of love; it offers only one way to think about love: the traditional one, belonging to the past. It used to be that marriage offered almost an ownership of the partner (more so for men than women). With a divorce rate of fifty percent, contraception, women's liberation and the state of the economy, the old myth can infect the psyche, a confusion of love with codependency. The

romantic fallacy has created a kind of harm similar to sex-
ism and racism; it is cultural garbage.

Unload some projections

Neuroscience confirms two realities evident to therapists:
the first is that our vulnerability cannot be avoided; the
second is that we have an extraordinary capacity to move
beyond instinctual programming, a capacity that neuroscience explains by the extreme plasticity of the human
brain. Neuroscience also supports the idea that it is not
so much our vulnerability that creates the problem, it is
the lack of exercise of the higher centers of the brain. In
other words it is not the *presence* of the croc and the pup
that turns heartbreak into a tragedy, but the *absence* of the
wise human. Wisdom, like happiness, cannot be reached
directly, only indirectly, by deletion of what stands in the
way. The art of becoming wiser is similar to the art of
gardening: one percent planting for ninety nine percent
weeding! Weeds come in a variety of species; passive-aggressive behaviors are one extremely invasive kind; projections are another.

Like passive-aggressive behaviors, we project onto the
partner as the result of our immature expectations about
love. You say "take your sweater off, I'm sweating" because you still have too much fusional desire. Neuroscientists found themselves compelled to use a concept

similar to the old psychoanalytic concept of *projection.* They call it *implicit memories,* but both concepts convey the sense that our adult relationships contain imprints of our earlier connections to the caretakers, in the form of neuronal circuits created in the past and still active in the brain.[41]

Those bundles of synapses were created in the past but they fire in the present. That fact is positive when the situation calls for responses that were learned in the past and are still adequate for the present. Having learned to fear the bite of one kind of venomous snakes helps you project the danger when you see a different kind of snake; your mistrust is then an adapted response.

If your grandpa was always making humiliating comments about your appearance, you may have learned to keep your distance from contemptuous personalities, a lesson from the past that still has value because there is no lack of mean people in the world. Staying away from them makes as much sense as avoiding venomous snakes. The problem starts when the automatic firing of neurons has no relevance to the present. If somebody tells you that you have a piece of lettuce stuck in your mustache and you feel a crushing sense of humiliation, you are not reacting to the present but to Grandpa. In such cases, *a new layer of connections* must be added to your repertoire, to delete unhelpful projections.

Neuroscience demonstrates how the fantastic plasticity of the human neocortex is responsible for humanity's resilience and progress. The threats from the environment and from relationships are constant, which is why we need to learn new ways. Neuroscientists all agree that ours is a *learn-or-perish* story. A culture, or a species, or an individual who refuse to learn inevitably declines.

Your recovery from heartbreak follows the same principle: either you transform your ways of relating to others, to yourself and to the world, or you become a dinosaur of love. The lessons learned in your past may not be relevant for the present. Psychologists use the term *unconscious projections* for what neuroscientists call *bundles of synaptic connections.* They are those lessons learned in the past; some are still valid, some are not.

The " bunddle" is activated in the experience of falling in love, because we first experience love (or the absence of it) in the family, when those connections are established in the brain. As an adult, it takes regular weeding to sort out which trait belongs to your actual partner and which to mom, or dad, or big sister, or mean grandpa.

Every man must discover for himself the lingering flavor of his mother complex. As long as he projects the Madonna onto his wife, he suffers from sexual inhibition. As long as he projects the infinitely Nurturing Mother Nature, he exhausts his wife and she may abandon such a heavy baby. A man in love will project beautiful Aphrodite, wise Athena, strong Artemis, Good Mother Nature, but if the load of projections is too heavy, disappointment is inevitable because no woman is a goddess.

The damage to a relationship is amplified when the projections are negative: the man who projects the Whore, or Lady Macbeth, or Evil Witch, or Devouring Mother has a hard time with his wife. The nature of the projection depends on the son's indelible experience of his mother. As a rule, a son who has had a good-enough connection to his mother has the best chances at succeeding with his partner. He knows his mother is not a goddess, but loves her anyway because his experience was overall positive.

The same is true for every woman: she must clean up the projections coming from her father complex before she can enjoy being a wife, lover, and friend. Almost every year, a female student will ask: "how is it that I turn all my lovers into my babies?" The blunt answer, that a teacher cannot deliver but that a therapist could, is quite obvious: "your projections honey; they are too strong, and you have too many. Unload some!"

In neurological parlance, projections are connections established in the past that fire up *automatically* in the present. When a woman turns her lovers into her babies, it is because she unconsciously *projects* her need for nurturance onto the partner, offering too much nurturance and not enough of the other ingredients-- such as friendship, or sex, or partnering. Her mate unconsciously oblige by taking what is offered and becomes the big baby, albeit only with her. When the husband has had enough maternal caretaking, he finds his true mate and leaves. "Thanks, Mom, for all the nurturance, now I am going to get myself a wife. Bye!" The wife is devastated. An equally tragic possibility is that the husband never leaves the infantile position and becomes a heavier and heavier big baby. That story line ends with the exhaustion of the caregiver and the rage of the big baby.

Persistent neurological networks that have created our habitual relational style cannot be modified without first becoming conscious, hence the benefit of therapy. It would be practical if our infantile projections emerged with one of those tags attached to electric devices: *Warning: do not plug any new relationship in the socket of your past wounding.* To complicate matters, the more traumatic the initial wounding, the more solid are the neurotic defenses, preventing any kind of updating.

A neurotic personality is one that keeps plugging actual connectors in a power outlet that delivers the energy of the infantile defenses. It produces shorts and shocks of variable intensity, which, sadly enough, feel better than no current at all. A neurotic defense feels more comfortable to the immature personality than the risk of spreading one's wings. Yet, in the long run, too much energy wasted in defense mechanisms destroys vitality. [42]

It may be stunning, even humiliating, to discover that your fear of losing the partner has an unconscious charge that comes from a resurgence of the infantile panicky self. "Me? A scared, dependent, vulnerable, preverbal, helpless, clingy, needy, unconscious little person? Yeaerk!" The discrepancy between your adult competent self and your regressed needy child is a painful but crucial insight. You have to *feel* and *re-experience*, in full cinematographic precision, how your panic is the similar to the one you experienced in infancy.

Defense mechanisms are as varied as individuals; one person's defense may be to become a pleaser, while another becomes an abuser. The idiosyncratic *style* in which you defend yourself is not as important as the fact that it is outdated, a costly waste of psychic energy that can go on for a lifetime. A neurotic defense starts as a good enough management of limited psychological resources, a coping strategy, which is why it is called a *defense* mechanism— it defends the vulnerable infantile psyche against dangerous emotional overload.

As children, we survive our vulnerability by *not* becoming aware of any fact that would be unbearable; we *dissociate* from reality when reality is unacceptable to the fragile psyche. A good trick! I still easily dissociate whenever I need to go for a painful medical procedure: "me, scared? Not at all, I am not even here!" A common example of the necessity of defense mechanisms is a child's reaction to the death of the primary caregiver. Young children do not—and *should not*—experience the full impact of such a loss.

I remember a six-year-old boy, whose mother had suddenly died of heart failure; at the funeral parlor, he behaved as if not concerned with all the fuss and the tears around him. He stayed prudently away from his distressed father, running around the buffet table at the memorial service, tasting everything and enjoying the attention as if it was his birthday party; he was disconnected, aloof and emotionally unreachable. It would have been overwhelming to realize the amplitude of his loss, so his brain offered the option to dissociate, disconnect, repress, ignore. Like a power bar with a surge protector, the psyche of a child automatically disconnects if the charge is dangerously high. Adults do it, too, albeit they can handle higher charges.

A defense mechanism becomes troublesome only later, when the child's worldview built at the time of the trauma is now blurring the vision of the present. For example, the child at the funeral parlor did not tell his dad: "I was a really bad boy yesterday, is it why mommy died?" But he had an uneasy feeling about having really annoyed his mom just hours before she died. This kind of faulty association might literally remain inscribed in the folds of the child's brain, and later manifest as neurotic guilt. The grown-up man who discovers that he has always equated being a bad boy with killing his mother might finally understand why, each time he hears the slightest criticism from his wife, he overreacts. "My wife expresses annoyance because I keep forgetting to take out the garbage and I hear that I am bad and killing her." His reaction is the essence of a projection, based on outdated bundles of synaptic connections firing *as in* the past.

Our adult relationships contain not only the past traumas, but also the potential for updating. As the weeding of projections progresses, the adult finally sees what the child could not: "mom didn't die because I was a bad boy, but because she had a bad heart. What a relief!" When that flowering of consciousness appears, the adult is ready to drop the neurotic defense and to respond with a more adapted behavior: "Oh, yes, the garbage, thanks for the reminder; I keep forgetting!" The trigger that brought out the outdated connection has been deactivated.

The task of retrieving projections provided the bread and butter for therapists for the past century, and will continue to do so, even if we rename them *pre-wired synaptic connections ready to fire*. The patient's task remains the same: to understand that the dissociation might have been lifesaving then and there, but is now a neurotic waste.

CHAPTER 4

AH! JEALOUSY

One of the most unpleasant emotions in the repertoire of humans is the feeling that somebody is trying to steal our 'love object.' No human being can claim to be completely free of jealousy because it comes with our instinctual territory. The crocodile says: "this is my lunch, and you won't get it!" The kitten says: "I'm fighting for the nipple, because if I can't get access to it, I'll die." Many a parent has heard their child declare with the utmost naturalness, "Mom, let's return the new baby to the hospital, I really don't find it all that fun." The child has to be *taught* to tolerate the frustration of having to share Mom's services.

A normal child instinctively understands that trashing the new baby may threaten the essential connection to Mom! Even an only child will experience jealousy: "If Mom has other priorities besides precious little me, such as sex with Dad, friends she likes to entertain, the advancement of her career, books she likes to read . . . it may signal danger; she might forget me; I might be abandoned; I'll die." Freud theorized the mother's breast as the initial *love object*, a concept that aptly names the infantile *objectification* of the provider of pleasure. But in doing so, he also sexualized the whole story with his Oedipal theory. Neuroscience undoes the Freudian theory by insisting that it is a pre-sexual issue of survival, in other words a crocodile and puppy issue!

Rivalry can be a factor of evolution

The word *rival* originally meant two people living on opposite sides of the same river. The word for bank in French is 'rive' and "rivalry" is what happens when both sides fight for the same resource: water, milk, food, territory, money, love, sex, whatever is coveted by both sides. Unfair taxation, political injustices, family feuds, all have the same archetypal quality: move over so I can access the resource. The expression *the milk of human kindness*, which is synonymous with compassion, is one of the oldest metaphors equating the breast with everything that one may need to survive. Jealousy and rivalry are as ancient as the history of humanity and as inevitable, because of the survival instinct combined with the scarcity of some resources.

A rival who takes all the milk from the breast, all the water from the river, all the food from the cellar, all the dollars from the account, all the tax money from the state, threatens the survival of the less powerful ones. Jealousy has been called the oldest sin in the world, because the temptation to eliminate the rival spares no one. Jealousy is first felt as a physical reptilian urge, and then it spreads in the limbic brain as a generalized panic. If the education of the young is faulty, or if the law is biased against one group or one gender, or if the so-called neurons in the moral brain[43] have been destroyed, the ethical brakes are not there to stop jealous acting out. Jealousy then becomes one of the darkest zones of the human heart.

Nietzsche's admiration for the moral genius of the Greeks had to do not only with their recognition of the dark sentiments like jealousy but also with their capacity to upgrade those sentiments into something that has value. Ancient Greek wisdom suggested that the best revenge against jealousy is to do better than the competitor. For example, if the rival community takes an unfair amount of the water, it may propel a community to invent the technique of drilling a well, which eventually gives them better access to water than before. Are we fighting for oil? Let's invent alternative energy sources that will eventually bring more wealth. Are we fighting for territory? Let's explore techniques of desalinization to bring life to a desert. Are you fighting for love? It should push you to multiply the sources of love, develop some new abilities, transform your personality to become a less self-centered person, get a diploma, a promotion, a new apartment, outdo the competition.

Many historians have pointed out how issues of fairness in the use of the water in Ancient Mesopotamia was the motivation for the formulation of rules and regulations that evolved into one of the most sophisticated code to regulate the fair use of water. The sixth Babylonian king, Hammurabi, wrote this code in 1754 BC, and it remains among the oldest deciphered writings of significant length in the world. His code of law became a model for all civilizations. Mesopotamia means "the land between the two rivers" which means that people could access to the Tigris-Euphrates river system from four different banks! What began as a cause for lethal rivalry created the impetus for progress.

You don't own the partner

The institution of slavery, as well as the proprietary attitude toward women, both have a similar history. The law that forbids your neighbor from diverting the river has the same ultimate goal as the laws that prevent (or should prevent) a master from owning a slave, a husband from owning his wife and daughters as if they were his private property. The toleration of honor killings has nothing to do with honor; it indicates that the dominant gender inter-prets the concept of "honor" as the ownership of a chattel, like slaves owners used to do.

The moral goal has always been to supersede the croc-odile, supersede the puppy, and move to a person-to-per-son relationship, as opposed to a person-to-object rela-tionship. Unfortunately, not everyone on this planet has reached that level of moral development, confirming that moral values do follow a process of evolution, just like medical science or technology. The history of our dark sentiments shows how *all* progressive countries moved, or are moving, toward equalitarian laws on two parallel issues; one has to do with collective resources and the need to prevent employers, heads of state, politicians from behaving as if they owned the people, the land and the resources. The other issue where our laws are in con-stant evolution deals with private behaviors, to prevent husbands and parents from behaving as if they owned their wives and children.

Along with rationality and our propensity to think philosophically, to imagine artistically, to understand his-torically, the moral sense of the wise human is part of what we are all capable of as human beings. Anything that is part of our culture can be part of our psyche, the richer the culture of our community, the richer our psy-che! Consider this: jealousy is an emotion with a history.

The sentiment of jealousy used to be considered *un-controllable*, which is why crimes of passion (meaning husbands killing their unfaithful wives) were in the past routinely absolved. Jealousy has evolved into an emotion that is to be expected, but not one a civilized person should *act on*. If *we the people* can evolve by formulating laws that punish crimes of passion like any other crime, so can the individual caught in the jealous emotion.

Some cultures or nations are more advanced than others in this evolution, a discrepancy that is at the core of the argument in favor of a planetary culture, to preserve collective natural resources, limit procreation to a sustainable level, and protect the dignity of all human beings. Of course, we are not always acting according to our values; nonetheless, the moral direction is toward fairness in our code of law.

Beware of psychic inflation

When a rival deprives us of our object of love, our *feeling* can be a murderous one, but our *behavior* has to be otherwise. A lack of control of one's primitive feelings not only presents a risk of negative legal consequences, but it also harms what, in you, has the power to set you free. The jealousy instinct, like the arousal of primitive anger, leads to a psychic state that depth psychology describes as *psychic inflation*. The word *inflation*, when used about the economy, means an increase of currency or credit relative to the availability of goods and services, which eventually leads to higher prices and devaluation of that currency.

Carl Jung used the notion of inflation to mean a psychic state characterized by an exaggerated and unreal sense of one's importance, the cause of which is the identification of the subject with an archetypal image.[44] Jung's definition points at the confusion between the partner (the human, limited, fallible person who died, or who rejected you to go with another) and the archetypal Lover, to whom you give an inflated quasi-divine power.

We project on the Archetypal Lover the power of creation and destruction, of reward and punishment. Such inflation is a problem of the ego that always wants to amplify its importance, as if saying: I am that Divine Child in need of rescue, the Most Lovable Adult in the Cosmos, the Sweetest Person Ever to Exist, the Absolute Attractor of Love; how dare you reject this Sublime Person that is Me with a capital M? An inflated personality is someone who has regular indigestion of capital letters, a psychic ballooning! Any *invasion of unconscious contents* results in a puffing up of the ego and inevitably leads to a devaluation of the currency of love.

Those unconscious contents which invade the ego can be summarized in a brief formula: it is *everything you failed to mourn*, starting with the loss (or lack) of the exclusive attention of mommy dearest, daddy dearest, and all their surrogates.[45]

A relationship addiction is the same as a gambling addiction

This loss or lack happened in the past, but you never mourned the loss, so it invades you now. Just like the gambler who stays glued to the gaming table, convinced that he will recoup his loss and get lucky again, the jealous maniacal person keeps insisting for love's return. Indulging in an addiction always leads to disappointment and failure, yet the addict keeps doing it anyway. Gamblers *know* their addiction threatens their financial security, harms their relationships, destroys their health, but it does not stop them. Jealousy has similar features: it provokes an extravagant expenditure of psychic energy, with the certainty of failure.

In neuroscientific terms, jealousy is the result of the billions of synaptic connections that used to bond us first to mother, then to the partner, but now fail to elicit a reaction, making us as jealous as the five-year-old child who wants that new baby to go back where it came from. Neuroscience uses the term *neural memory* while depth psychology uses the terminology of an *invasion of unconscious contents,* or *unmourned losses.* Whatever one chooses to call it, *it* prevents us from experiencing the novelty of an adult relationship between two equal partners. The brain cannot develop new connections as long as we keep passively waiting for the same stimulation.

As Einstein is often quoted to have said: insanity consists in doing the same thing repeatedly while expecting a different result. Einstein's definition of madness is a good description of the obsessive and controlling behaviors stemming from jealousy: they do not inspire love, and always lead to the bankruptcy of the relationship.

There is a way *around* jealousy.

First, you have to *admit* jealousy. Second, as a preventive measure, it is prudent to tiptoe away from situations that provoke it. And third, it helps to develop the capacity to find pleasure in as many situations as possible. Developing multiple sources of pleasure is like digging a well when the river dries up, which ends scarcity. The process of diversification of pleasures starts with a curiosity for other things and other persons aside from the usual partner. Look at the places in you that are not connected to your ex-partner and spend time there.

Your ex did not like to read books but you do? Buy yourself a big fat novel and binge read. You like gardening but never had time for it? Go to the nursery and buy plants that will create the obligation to plant them. You used to cook for your partner? Send an email to friends:

"Will you come to dinner? I feel like trying this new recipe." Every time you do something new, synaptic associations get created, and soon replace the broken ones. Busy with new life, our attention moves away from the situation that provokes jealousy. Our brain needs its daily pleasure diet, and if the partner does not provide it any more, one has to change the menu.

Is it envy or jealousy?

Jealousy is a reaction to someone stealing what you feel is yours, be it your dinner, your money, your partner. Kids are fiercely jealous: this is my mommy, and I won't share! When your partner dies, nobody can take him/her away from you and you may think you are free from jealousy. Yet, the dark emotion often takes the form of a related emotion: envy. Kids too are prone to envy: "I want as many toys as you have. I want the same, I want all that you have, now." Envy is wanting everything the Jones have, and more.

The widowed is not jealous, but may feel envious: "why did I lose my partner to death while they still have theirs?" The emotion of envy needs to be treated just like that of jealousy: don't beat yourself for feeling it, recognize it and *take your distance* from the crocodile and the needy baby. The jealousy or envy reflex can never be erased from the brain because we are vulnerable to loss of love. Nevertheless, just as the building of positive addictions is the most powerful strategy against destructive addictions, another set of reactions can supersede the destructive emotions. "Ok, I am having a fit of envy! I summon the wise human in me, to bring calm. I walk, breathe, look around, and let go of my ego obsession of wanting to control Madam Death!"

CHAPTER 5

RELATIONSHIP ADDICTION

Your Beloved was the sun, the moon, the North Star, the home base. Together, you wrote the script, directed the action, funded the production, created the set, and enjoyed the mutual applause.

Then, the Beloved left and handed you the pink slip: "thank you very much, I won't need your services any more. I am taking my story in another direction, please leave the stage and recede into the dark." You are left with the task of sorting out what is an essential part of your identity, and what belongs to the identity you had with your partner. It takes one thing and its opposite: tranquility and silence to rebuild a sense of self, but it also takes connecting to others, to test the new identity.

A teenager who spends most of his or her time collecting hundreds of friends on Facebook expresses the natural agony of not yet being somebody; heartbreak brings on a psychological vacuity similar to that of the isolated teenager suffering from *relationship addiction* and spinning in the void in front of the screen. An incapacity to appreciate your solitude leads to relationship addiction as quickly as an incapacity for intimacy leads to isolation.

Since the ancient Greeks, not much has been written about the psychology of *mental health,* because our psychiatry and psychology emerged from the medical model of *mental sickness*, whereas the Greeks' notion of mental health emerged from their philosophy about the good life. We could borrow at least one of their basic principles: mental health is equilibrium. For example, if our natural disposition is gloomy, the Greek wisdom might suggest that one should balance it by developing a comic and rosier imagination of life's dramas. The genre of comedy can be a valid counterweight to a melancholic disposition. Conversely, if our natural disposition is romantic and naïve, wisdom would recommend the study of history or involvement in politics.

If you trust the Greek principle of balancing opposites, it means that if your social diet contains too much solitude, balance it with more relating; but if you suffer from agitation, consumerism, relationship addiction, go for a silent retreat. Traditional Chinese philosophy has a similar definition of health: a balance or *harmony* between the yin and the yang. The notion of Tao is a term that translates as *the path*; it describes the basic unity of life as one of balance between poles.

The values that today govern education rarely include an appreciation of solitude and silence. I find it sad because the capacity to love implies comfort with one's own quiet company. A school system (or a family) that never allows kids silence and solitude create a neurotic addiction to relationships, to being seen, heard and applauded. The more the addiction contaminates love, the more love disappoints. This neurotic aspect of symbiotic love has to be dealt with sooner or later, and heartbreak is the best occasion to master the art of solitude/silence.

The realm of the invisible

With heartbreak, there is a moment when you have to accept that, for the present time, you are temporarily but truly *invisible*. Invisibility of the kinds that peasants, serfs, slaves, servants, have had to endure at the hands of their masters. Black characters in most of the nineteenth century American literature were invisible; the story was not about them, but about the white masters. A child in an abusive household is not seen, not heard. The low paid, untrained, disposable employee in a huge organization is invisible. Older women today are invisible. You must accept the fact that you are now the ghost of the person you were, you are invisible.

An ex-nun told me she asked the chaplain of her community why the matriarchs in the Bible did not get as elaborate stories as the patriarchs. He didn't have an answer; and she concluded that in patriarchal religions, women are not seen, not heard, and their concerns and questions remain unanswered: they are invisible. As a heartbroken person, know that you inhabit the realm of the invisible and make your peace with the fact.

Our identity is built through our connection to other human beings. Even the lonesome scientist, working in his lab eighty hours a week, gets his sense of self from a vocation that *in itself* connects him to the rest of humanity. One can be married to science, married to a mission, married to a cause and these loners, although not connected to a conjugal partner, are connected to humanity. They can lead beautiful, generous lives, although their pursuit is solitary. Introverted artists, solo explorers, Carmelites, nuns, reclusive monks are not necessarily misanthropes. Like Saint Francis of Assisi, one can walk alone in the woods, talking to the birds, and reach the spiritual summit that is the feeling of our essential connectedness. Our relationship to others takes multiple forms, yet it cannot exist without a capacity to remain in solitude.

Because of heartbreak, your capacity to enjoy solitude must be exercised anew, like walking on a leg that has been in a cast for a long time. The feeling of largesse, which comes from being at ease in the world, needs time to grow in a healing heart.

Heartbreak is a triple loss

At first, the physical absence of the partner seems like the only cause of our suffering and one is under the illusion that if he or she would only come back, all would be fine again. It is truly an illusion because there are three absentees in the drama of heartbreak.

The first is the beloved, and even if that person were to come back, the second absentee, the person you were *with* the beloved, and the third absentee, the person you were *for* the beloved, are never coming back. This triple loss explains the loss of a sense of identity. Individuals suffering heartbreak have nightmares of losing their nametag, passport, car keys, of being lost in a strange city, of walking in a cemetery and reading their name on a funeral monument, of having no voice, no head, no body, of coming to work and somebody else's name is on the door of their office, or coming home and their mother asks them to introduce themselves... all are metaphors of an estrangement from the self. The only solution is to become somebody else.

One aspect of our need for love is its role in the development of identity. It starts as infants and never stops: "Look, Mom, I can walk. Look, Dad, I can ride my bike.

Look, teacher, I got that equation right. Look, professor, here is my dissertation. Look, partner, here is the product of my work." The basic contract between parent and child involves all aspects of identity building: physical, psychological, social. Every child comes to this life with the same message: "I am young, fragile, and I need your love to define me. I'll try to be whoever you want me to be, in exchange for your care and security." Psychologists have written volumes about the role of parents in the formation of the child's emerging self.

Philosophers have argued that our identity is a psychosocial construct, a compromise between what our parents want, what society wants, and what we think we want. Since identity is a construct, it follows that is can be deconstructed. The myth of the divine rights of kings is a perfect example of a deconstructionist attack on a value that was no longer sustainable.

Heartbreak is a similar demolition derby of an obsolete identity. The lover, a mirror who used to reflect a positive image of yourself, now reflects nothing, or if it does, it is a tarnished, ugly picture that communicates, "sorry, but you are no longer adequate." The identity built to attract and relate to the partner is a dead cable connector. Heartbreak is such a rough deconstruction that it is felt at first like a death of the self. There is a word for that feeling: *alienation,* which means a *separation from oneself.*

In the Middle Ages, the word *alienation* was synonymous with madness, the caricature of it being the lunatic patient who has so little sense of self, he thinks he is Christ or a bird who can fly from the tenth story of the building. Sociologists later used the word *alienation* to describe any situation where the sense of self—collective or personal—is lost.

For example, peasants coming to find work in the city and losing their connections to their ancestral house, culture, and mores, were said to feel alienated. Karl Marx used the word *alienation* to mean the loss of meaning in one's life, when the work does not contribute to the sense of self. The loss of your partner is one of the most alienating events. You may still know your name and still perform at work, yet your core identity is shaken, the mirror broken.

You have to ask yourself the following question: "if I cannot be who I was, who can I become?" Invent, discover, imagine, try, and become that new person.

Chapter 6

Narcissism: a trend and a curse

The breakup of an intimate relationship is a huge narcissistic wound, maybe the most acute of adult life. Issues of narcissism—your own as well as your partner's—are a crucial aspect of the process of rehabilitation, because narcissism tends to limit to a purely utilitarian nature the exchanges one has with the world, as well as with others. We easily accept that a burn victim experiencing severe pain will be concerned mainly with his or her own suffering; the professional caretakers don't expect otherwise.

But our patience with the egocentricity of the sick or handicapped partner eventually wears out. Even the most generous heart will tire of a partner's handicap, of his/her story of past trauma, his/her fragile condition. It is called compassion fatigue and it harms the connection. But when a person uses everybody's compassionate heart to get more than his or her faire share, it is called narcissism.

Heartbreak burns like hell and you expect compassion from others. You feel as if our heartbreak is the worst in human history, exceptional, unique, when it fact it is an archetypal, universal experience. You have to be careful not to stay in this egocentric mode for too long.

Narcissism does to the psyche what a monoculture does to the environment. The monoculture of me, me and more me, creates an impoverishment that leads to devastation. The tradition at a wake is to bring food and support to the bereaved because a healthy community understands that the pain of the bereaved calls for compassion. Yet, if the widow or widower remains, year after year, in the sad and egocentric emotions brought about by the loss, that person risks another loss: the connection to the community.

It is as if the mourner is saying: "only my suffering counts, yours is nothing compared to mine." It may indicate what psychiatry calls a Narcissistic Personality Disorder, which describes somebody who is narcissistic all the time, with everybody, in all situations.

Therapists know that one of the most difficult task is to help a narcissist see his/her narcissism; in my whole career as a psychologist and therapist few patients were able to tackled their narcissism. But it is not impossible, especially after repeated failures of relationships.

Susan was an adult student studying to get her Ph.D. in psychology, a training she started quite late in her life because her first career was as an actress. At fifty, she discovered that the proportion of roles for older women in Hollywood was the reverse of the sociological reality. After a period of despair, she trained for a degree in psychology. As part of the curriculum, she was expected to develop two basic skills: *empathy* and *listening*—at which she consistently failed. She discovered that she really could not grasp any of the emotions, feelings, or body language expressed by the classmates with whom she did the exercises. She was despairing about her future as a psychotherapist when she had a transforming experience.

One day, a student in the class became so annoyed with her incapacity to listen to others, that she lashed out at her: "Susan, you are such a narcissist! And you are such a drama queen! I can't team up with you any more." At the break, Susan went into the library, to read the definition of the Narcissistic Personality Disorder (DSM IV. 301.81).

It reads: "A pervasive pattern of grandiosity (in fantasy or behavior), a need for admiration, and a lack of empathy, beginning by early adulthood and present in a variety of contexts, as indicated by five (or more) of the following nine criteria:

(1) has a grandiose sense of self-importance (e.g., exaggerates achievements and talents, expects to be recognized as superior without commensurate achievements);

(2) is preoccupied with fantasies of unlimited success, power, brilliance, beauty, or ideal love;

(3) believes that he or she is special and unique and can only be understood by, or should associate with, other special or high-status people (or institutions);

(4) requires excessive admiration;

(5) has a sense of entitlement, i.e., unreasonable expectations of especially favorable treatment or automatic compliance with his or her expectations;

(6) is interpersonally exploitative, i.e., takes advantage of others to achieve his or her own ends;

(7) lacks empathy: is unwilling to recognize or identify with the feelings and needs of others;

(8) is often envious of others or believes that others are envious of him or her;

(9) shows arrogant, haughty behaviors or attitudes".

She had been told many times before that she was a
drama queen. She then read the category 301.50 of the
DMS IV, the *Histrionic Personality Disorder* (which used
to be called a *hysterical personality* in prior editions of
the DSM and corresponds to the popular notion of drama
queen.) The *Histrionic Personality Disorder* has many
traits in common with *Narcissistic Personality Disorder,*
but has more emphasis on the need for intensity and attention (the drama queen.) The eight diagnostic criteria are
the following:

(1) is uncomfortable in situations in which he or
   she is not the center of attention;

(2) interaction with others is often characterized
   by inappropriate sexually seductive or provoc-
   ative behavior;

(3) displays rapidly shifting and shallow expression of emotions;

(4) consistently uses physical appearance to draw
   attention to self;

(5) has a style of speech that is excessively impres-
   sionistic and lacking in detail;

(6) shows self-dramatization, theatricality, and exaggerated expression of emotion;

(7) is suggestible, i.e. easily influenced by others
or circumstances;

(8) considers relationships to be more intimate
than they actually are."

Susan was in shock and that shock helped her discover her narcissistic and histrionic traits. She decided to learn a different way of relating to people. Five years after leaving the school, with her psychology degree, I met her at a conference and we talked about the day she looked at herself through the categories of the DSM. I asked her if we could tape an interview and here is my summary of it.

The rage of a baby

Every one of my partners left me saying more or less the same thing: that I am impossible to live with! It took me a degree in psychology and years of therapy to see that I was indeed self-obsessed and hysterical.

Had I been less physically attractive and not in the acting profession, I might have discovered my problem earlier. I lived most of my life with a constant need for intravenous drips of adoration, and as an actress I got it.

Being fed a high dosage of devotion only intensified my need, like a sugar addiction that makes you crave sweets. Directors, camera men, sound technicians, makeup artists, all got used to complimenting me regularly; otherwise I would get too nervous to perform.

The world was my stage and my life a performance to receive applause. I didn't have eyes to see, only to check if I was seen.

When I was six years old, I was already looking at myself in shop windows and claiming my parent's attention every minute of the day —and getting it. At forty, just before losing the good looks that kept me employed as an actress, I had become completely intoxicated with a daily dose of "you look stunning, radiant, luminous, glorious, breathtaking, glowing, extraordinary."

The only living creatures in my intimacy were my dog and my two cats. I had no friends, only fans. I would round every situation to keep center stage: all eyes on me, my problems, my aches, my success, my needs; me at the center of everything, me the nicest flower of the bouquet, me forever planting my flag in the middle of every territory. I was blind, deaf, dumb to others, to all but me, and me again, and me all the time.

I lived with the rage, the fear, the need of the child I had been. I was my mother's doll, her toy, her claim to fame, her compensation for a life unlived. I worked hard to become a star and I succeeded, only to discover, at 50, the big mistake that had made me think that having the adoration of a crowd would make me love myself. Mistake!

What I needed to change was the way I treated others, and not the way I looked in a mirror. When I began studying to become a psychologist, what really helped me was the discipline of listening to patients. I learned an openness to others that still is a daily miracle for me.

A rejection from the partner can be a reminder that narcissism is a dangerous ego-intoxication that needs to be treated on a regular basis. Had Susan decided not to hear the feedback from her classmates, her story would have turned into the typical sad ending of aging narcissists: social isolation. Nature is always giving us lessons about what is sustainable, and what is not. Narcissistic relationships are the ultimate example of unsustainability.

The diagnosis of narcissism was very popular in the seventies and eighties, with Christopher Lasch's denunciation of how our education system and family values breed narcissism.[46] Yet, this denunciation did not have much impact on societal policies, maybe because of Lasch's suggestion that narcissism was the result of a decline in religious practice, a theory proven wrong by further analysis. In psychology, the attention went elsewhere, and the category of Borderline Personality Disorder replaced Narcissistic Personality Disorder as the trendy diagnosis; one could be a narcissist again and nobody would notice.[47]

Fads exist in psychiatry, which means that a new diagnostic category offers the possibility to see something new, but also to *not see* something else, once the spotlight has moved away.

Post-Freudian theorists such as Lacan and Kohut had a more enduring influence than Lasch, yet their ideas were expressed in a heavy jargon that was a deterrent to many. I prefer the earlier, blunt, simple affirmations by Freud and Jung, that an adult is somebody who failed to evolve *beyond* the primary narcissism of the child who rages at having to share mom's services.

The widespread phenomenon of adults who won't grow up now has as much a cultural cause as a clinical one. As a result of the general tolerance for successful narcissists, many adults expect a caretaking that should not be expected past infancy. The narcissist is never satisfied with what life has to offer, always expecting more, more, more, an emotional bulimia. Our cultural diet is too rich in sweet romance, tolerance for self-inflicted victim-hood, and too poor in salty wisdom.

Heartbreak naturally brings about many ugly traits of the clinical portrait of the narcissist. First, there is that grandiose sense of self-importance, because you feel your loss is like no one else's: more profound, more painful and exceptional. You are absorbed in yourself and temporarily cannot hear or see others. Most of all, you suffer from a narcissistic sense of *entitlement* that is a natural regressive pull: you feel as if the partner *owes* you love because parents owe love to the child.

Learn to smell a narcissist

If your breakup is due to the narcissism of your partner and you ended the relationship out of exhaustion, your breakup is still a narcissistic wound for your ego. It may seem easy to break up a relationship with a selfish, self-serving, egocentric, navel-gazing, egomaniacal tak-er, yet many decent individuals get caught in their net. You need to learn how to recognize and avoid narcissists.

In the beginning of a relationship a narcissist can be very seductive, seemingly warm, receptive, and generous. He or she might be rich, or famous, good looking, popular in your milieu or powerful in the organization you work for. The attention of such a social star feeds you own, nat-ural enough, narcissistic needs.

The hook is always your need for attention, and the narcissist's most clever trick is to use this need as bait to trap you in a one-way partnership. The fact that narcissism is culturally so well tolerated does not help us to recognize it, especially in milieus where star status is a core value. Narcissistic parents tend to transmit their narcissistic traits to their kids, which means that as long as the family has the means to maintain a position of social dominance, the parents and their kids can be as narcissistic as they please, and nobody will object. Their failure to love is not perceived because love is a private emotion, its absence not obvious to the Joneses, or to the media.

There are now two major theories about narcissism, one from psychoanalysis and the other from social psychology. They seem to contradict each other, but I think they are both relevant when deciding which form of narcissism one is dealing with.

The first theory is the classical Freudian psychoanalytic perspective, which distinguishes between the so-called *primary narcissism* (the normal self-centeredness of the child) as opposed to *secondary narcissism*, which today would be called a healthy self-esteem. Both these forms of narcissism are part of human nature: primary narcissism is to be expected in children and adolescents; secondary narcissism in the adult personality, represents the natural need to be seen and appreciated. Wanting to have a haircut that makes you look good is an example of healthy secondary narcissism.

In Freud's view, when primary narcissism persists beyond adolescence, it signals a failure to fit in the give-and-take mode of adult life, as well as a failure of love. In the generations of Freudian followers, a plethora of psychoanalysts (Kohut,[48] Horney,[49] Masterson,[50] Milton,[51]) theorized pathological narcissism as the result of *self-loathing.* The narcissistic personality, in their view, is a defense mechanism against a narcissistic wounding in childhood.

In a nutshell, the narcissist inflates his or her value as compensation for feeling worthless: "I make myself too big because I feel too small." A more recent theory about narcissism paints a totally different portrait of the narcissist. He or she is no longer the *self-loathing individual* of early psychoanalysis, but a *self-adoring individual* [52]*, the* result of a culture that rewards takers and tolerates bullying. I think both these perspectives can be relevant because there is more than one brand of narcissism, another voracious plant that spreads like weeds and can grow on both grounds.

If you are recovering from breaking up with a narcissist, it is useful to examine those two theories in detail, and see which one fits your ex-partner, and which one fits your own overgrown narcissism, in order to remove the hook that attracted you to such a taker.

The narcissist as a *self-loathing* individual

Psychoanalytic theory first's intention was to reverse the nineteenth century perceptions by stating that a narcissist is *not* someone who loves himself or herself; it is someone who *does not know how to love*, showing neither love of self nor love of other.

The narcissist painted by psychoanalysis is cold to himself or herself, as well as to the partner, because he or she is still caught in the infantile rage against the parent whose approval and support was so needed, yet withheld. It is an individual incapable of *giving* —"I did not get what I needed, why should you?" If there were a bumper sticker to summarize the psychoanalytic theory about narcissism, it might read: *I am a narcissist. My curse is a hatred of what I most need: you.*

Heinz Kohut's book *The Analysis of the Self: A Systematic Analysis of the Treatment of the Narcissistic Personality Disorders* had a most significant impact in psychiatry because his definition of the narcissistic personality disorder found its way into the DSM. To become healthy adults, Kohut theorized, children needed to be *mirrored positively by an empathically resonant self-object*—by which he meant a family in which you feel valued, with competent adults who can be role models. If you are not properly *mirrored*, to use his jargon, you catch a narcissistic personality disorder.

The cure, according to Kohut, is to find a therapist who can take the place of the parent and, through transference, *re-parent* the patient. As the patient experiences a secure attachment with the therapist, he or she develops a coherent personality structure by repeated experiences of being *mirrored* (seen, valued).

Kohut imagines the ideal parent/therapist as someone who responds to the needs of the child/patient with a *"non-hostile firmness and a non-seductive affection."* Kohut's insistence on the importance of empathy in therapy came from his critique of the Freudian frame of reference. Kohut was born in Vienna in 1913 and wrote his major work from the fifties to the seventies. Kohut frame of reference was strictly clinical; he did not take into account the growth of cultural narcissism, and did not comment on the actual dismal failure to provide a *non-hostile firmness* in education; our educators are not *firm* and the schools are *hostile*. As usual, he put all the responsibility on the parenting, none on education and cultural values.

Kohut's theory dominated the field of psychoanalytic studies for a generation, although there were some sharp critics. One such criticism is that of James Hillman, who sees Kohut's approach to narcissism as a trap for patients.

He writes, "I keep a distance from the Kohut craze. Although recognizing narcissism as the syndrome of the times [. . .] Kohut attempts its cure by the same means of narcissistic obsession: an ever more detailed observation of subjectivity. And a subjectivity within the oppressive confines of a negatively reconstructed childhood."[53] Kohut's patients, says Hillman, become ever more fascinated by their story of childhood trauma, giving less and less attention to others and to the world, always in search of somebody to *mirror* them. The result is a crowd of individuals not looking at each other, but looking in mirrors.

The narcissist as a *self-adoring* individual

Starting with Christopher Lasch and his book *The Culture of Narcissism* (1979), the portrait of a narcissist became very different. Presented not as a victim of poor parenting and wounded self-image, the narcissist was for Lasch the result of a culture that cultivates the virus of narcissism as a virtue.

Social psychology[54] recently offered new and convincing evidence that the narcissist can be somebody truly *in love with himself* and *only* himself, a going back to the nineteenth century meaning of the word narcissism, this time from a sociological angle rather than a psychological one. This contemporary view of narcissism is based on a cultural critique of parents raising children like royalty ("what would you like to eat for dinner, honey?") and it comprises a critique of the economy, which offers credit cards to teenagers and to adults who themselves can't control their spending.[55]

That brand of narcissism, characterized by a lack of self-control, is theorized as the result of culture who wrongly believes that giving accolades *raises self-esteem* and *leads to success,* when research proves that it doesn't; in fact, it seems to be quite the opposite.

Summarizing years of research, by themselves and other social psychologists, Twenge and Campbell[56] describe the narcissist as somebody who:

1) really loves him or her/self first (*self-adoration,* really;)

2) feels entitled way beyond his or her competence;

3) is a handicap for a business because he or she is not a good team worker;

4) hurts those who commit themselves to him or her because he or she will use and abuse friends, co-workers, and spouses;

5) and finally, he or she becomes a pathetic, isolated loser when he or she loses good looks, or money, or a power position. This kind of nar-

cissism is presented as the natural outcome of
a consumerist culture that disconnects freedom
from responsibility. Immature parents let their
kids get away with irresponsibility because
they neurotically *need to be needed* and to feel
approved and loved by their kids, a reversal of
the past ideal of children striving for their parents' love and approval.

If you broke up with a pathological narcissist, it might
be useful to figure out which of these two contradictory
theories applies to your former partner. The *self-loathing*
narcissist has an inner voice that whispers: "anyone who
wants to be with me must not be worth loving".

It is exhausting to interact with a hungry, bottomless
wounded ego that gobbled every drop of emotional honey you can produce, while at the same time devaluing it
as worthless. Examine your need to be needed, question
your attraction to wounded puppies, try tough love, stop
wanting to be invisible.

If your partner was of the other kind, a *self-adoring*
narcissist, he or she asked you to play the role of the responsible supportive parent, while remaining the spoiled,
irresponsible teen, with the credit card and no responsibilities. Could it be that you never learned that fairness and
justice comes before love? Who taught you that love can
exist when one gives while the other takes?

Learn to smell the brats who disguise themselves as Prince Charming. Learn to detect spoiled little girls who disguise themselves as Love Goddesses. Typically, at the beginning of a relationship with a self-adoring narcissist, there is a period where you might have felt courted with extraordinary dedication. The narcissist's courtship is modeled on his or her own immature ideal of love: romance, gifts, glitter, ego flattering adulation.

Gradually, so gradually you may not have seen it coming, the wooing turned into a grand existential theft, and the partner performed a greedy appropriation of everything in your personality that could serve his or her needs. Your *self-adoring* partner, stuck in the infantile position of wanting much while contributing little, assigned to you the parental role of caretaker, but with *no reciprocity.*

It is an illusion to think that your generosity and devotion can transform an immature partner into someone capable of returning love. The self-adoring narcissist who has not yet learned to love is *not interested* in learning how to have a non-utilitarian relationship. "Don't bother me, and take care of all the problems" is the basic tune and your generosity confirms his or her sense of entitlement. An eternal adolescent (the "puer aeternus" described by Mary Louise von Franz[57]) will use the partner's resources as long as there is money and honey and will leave your with an broken heart, a dried up soul and an empty bank account.

Both theories of narcissism, either the self-loathing of psychoanalysis or the self-loving of social psychology, converge in the admission that narcissism is one of the most difficult problem to tackle. Love can only exist between equals, but for narcissists, the notion of equality remains mysterious.

When a narcissist is in the presence of authentic love between two people, he or she cannot grasp it. Narcissists cannot find love because they don't know what they are looking for. They have learned that being loved is equivalent to being serviced, like a car in a garage, a man at a bordello, a client on the massage table, a patient at the therapist, a customer at the restaurant. The cultural tolerance of narcissism has created hordes of people with bottomless needs and vampiristic psyches, a sociological phenomenon that may explain this generation's fascination with vampire stories. A narcissist is a vampire.

The trophy partner: narcissism by another name

> *It is a great happiness, because it is a private happiness. Modesty defends every intimacy. (Gaston Bachelard, Les Rêveries du Repos).*

The healthy narcissistic component in every relationship—Freud's notion of *secondary narcissism*—makes us want our partner, our kids, our parents, our friends, even our boss and our organization to reflect positively on ourselves. It is pleasant, when we buy our first house, to give a tour of it to our friends, feathers all fluffed up and gobbling compliments. It is natural to appreciate trophies, applauses, rewards, medals, compliments, honors and promotions. Rewards help us perform, win and excel. But we have to be careful that in some professions (politics, cinema…) narcissism is a work related ailment that is difficult to avoid.

It embarrassing to see how stars will put on a show of modesty (one of the preferred acts of stars) only as long as the camera is running. The real test of a healthy personality is in the context of intimacy. The notion of a 'trophy partner' defines a relationship that is all for show. The narcissist's display of interest in the trophy partner has very little to do with love: the partner is an item to show off to the admiring crowd. Stendhal called it *vanity love* because that is what it is: vanity.

The narcissist's primary relationship is not to the partner, but to those others who have the power to grant status. One indicator of a narcissistic partner is the way indifference replaces excitement as soon as the partners find themselves in private. An intimate relationship doesn't happen on stage, which is why a narcissist lover doesn't understand the value of intimate conversations, of intimate sex, of intimate anything. To say it philosophically, to be considered like a trophy *objectifies* the person. As a trophy partner, you are a prop in the narcissist's show. In order to have a couple, or a team, persons have to be persons, not objects.

The next vignette is about a woman who called herself a serial lover, because she had a great capacity to seduce, but not to sustain a long-term relationship. When she began reflecting on herself, she did not like the person she discovered. Veronica's suicidal impulse and detestation of herself was the trigger for a needed deconstruction of her narcisistic identity.

Monica, the frigid beauty queen

At eighteen, I won a national beauty contest. It brought me many marriage proposals. I married the guy with the money. He believed that a beauty queen like myself must automatically have a warm heart and a welcoming body.

He paid dearly for his illusion. For me, life was never about love, nor sex, but rather about survival. I am programmed to function in only one mode: problem-solving.

I have a sensual deficit. Other people around me seem to find pleasure in existing; they celebrate life, appreciate friends, fun, food; they have pleasure doing things with their loved ones.

The only way I can relate to anyone is to solve his or her problems. I need to be needed. I was sexually frigid with all my lovers, and also with the three men I married. The third husband is divorcing me for that same reason.

I am supposedly good looking, sexually technically functional, but I don't feel much and I guess they feel I can't feel!

I knew a woman, a friend of my mother, who was married to a successful and rich narcissist; she believed being a trophy was just fine, "my husband values me more than his Maserati". Her satisfaction lasted as long as the value put on her, as trophy, was high enough. Being considered an *object* of great value both revealed and satisfied her narcissistic traits. Individuals who are mostly "trophy partners" usually don't get depressed at being an object, only at being a *devalued* object. It is a sad story with a multitude of variations on the same theme: a man marries a beauty queen, she becomes pregnant, her body changes, she loses her looks and he loses interest in his trophy.

She then feels like garbage. Her heartbreak can be the occasion to become a person. A woman marries a man because of his ability to make money; the money dries up and the wife stops caring for him; he feels cheated and becomes violent. His heartbreak can be the occasion to find other values besides money. A child prodigy wins a Chopin contest at twenty but decides to become a dentist and his narcissistic mother shuns him. His heartbreak can be the occasion to discover who he is as a person, apart from his mother's projections. Here is how a young man, the son of a friend, was able to smell the odor of the partner's narcissism on a cashmere coat.

The cashmere label

Early in our relationship, my girlfriend gave me a very expensive black cashmere coat. She wanted be to tell everybody at work that it was her gift to me.

But I had ask her to keep our relationship a secret because my supervisor is a jealous type who tried to seduce her. I would lose my job if he were to find out. Nevertheless, she kept insisting that our love was worth the risk (by which she meant the risk of losing my job.) I was supposed to "honor" our relationship enough to make it public.

Yet in private, she was not so hot about me, as if our relationship was to be either a public affair or not at all! In public, she acted as if I was a good catch, but in private she had very little desire for sexual intimacy.

The more she insisted on our coming out as partners, the more I recoiled from it, until I broke up with her. I gave her back the cashmere coat, to give to her next glorious catch.

A culture of consumerism is a growing ground for successful narcissists, because there are plenty of financial rewards for those who can treat persons like things. There is no shortage of individuals who are willing to remain in a miserable marriage with a narcissist, for reasons of money or power. Their marriage is a business contract: "I'll cater to your needs, as long as you pay for the services."

Objectification of the Other is not something new; servants and slaves in racist societies have been or still are treated as objects, of more or less value, depending on their capacity to serve the master's needs and ambitions. The narcissist's message is clear: "your value increases or decreases according to your ability to serve my needs." There is nothing new, either, in the old strategy of youth and beauty marrying into wealth or nobility; it is not for love, but for power.

The difference with today's culture of consumerism rests in the *clarity* of the deal. When the contract is based on a conscious choice, an honest relationship can still exist. Whether the deal is money buying a name, or a name attracting money, or money buying youth, a deal is a deal, and it can be a fair deal. Many a romantic courtship is a polite concealment for the commercial nature of the contract.

The perversion is not so much in the deal, as in the ignorance of the real nature of the transaction. Balzac's novels describe many of the romantic baits used by ambitious young men, in order to attract the gullible girl with a big dowry. Balzac describes the romantic show of love as the honey to attract the bee. The girl's parents, to protect her, typically negotiate back and forth, through un-romantic lawyers, to draft the financial aspect of the marriage deal.

In Balzac's dramas, when the girl, now a wife, discovers that she was sold, her response is often to take a lover, to be a person at least with somebody. Balzac excelled at sociological realism: mix money with romance, ambition with naïveté and you have a balzacian plot.

When partners are not naïve, and are aware and willing to marry for other reasons than love, it is just that: a very ancient form of human transaction, not a narcissistic personality disorder, not a fraud. Many power couples today are alliances based on values that have more to do with power (social positioning) than with romantic attraction. Respect is a frequent outcome of the clarity of their deal.

Franklin D. Roosevelt had his romantic and sexual affairs on the side, yet he knew that Eleanor was his true partner in the social and family realm; her political opinions were precious to FDR. She developed her own deep friendships on the side.[58] The same is true of many an admirable couple, and it takes our culture's obsession with the romantic myth and sexual obsession, to remain blind to the value of such a conscious deal. The psychological damage begins not with the deal, but rather *with the unconsciousness* about the nature of the deal. It is the gullible innocence that is the problem, not the contractual nature of a relationship.

Many an immature women, attracted to power (usually in the form of money or fame,) expect the relationship to deliver incompatible benefits. Once married to the rich, ambitious, workaholic husband, the innocent wife starts complaining about the husband's lack of warmth, his incapacity for intimacy, not aware that it shows her own narcissistic position of wanting to have a husband who is a wolf with competitors, and a lamb with her.

The same unconsciousness characterizes the tragic figure of the older man who refuses to see that his very young, very beautiful, very sexy and very ambitious trophy wife is not really attracted to him, but to his money, and that she has a hidden agenda. Again, the problem is not so much in the deal but as in most interpersonal conflicts, in the incapacity to *see through* the darker aspects of the self. What is unbearable is not the contractual term of the relationship, which can be fair, but the emotional falsehood on which it rests.

Everything that is for sale is visible, on display, and has a price. Love is invisible, private—and if it can be bought, it's not love, which explains why it remains an inaccessible mystery to a narcissist. The narcissist excels at calculating cost/benefits, which is the ultimate ability in a consumerist culture, but one that does not apply to transactions of the heart.

A philosopher looking at the drama of narcissism might define the problem as such: the self is *not a thing*; neither are love, soul, and joy. The tragedy of the narcissist is that he or she can only relate to things, not persons.[59] Their need for social success is the need to be a valuable *thing* in the eyes of others. To be a valuable object in the eyes of another narcissist, or to have nice things that others can envy can never make up for the void at the core of the narcissist's personality. In terms of relating to others, the narcissist's options are reduced to a binary choice: a) the Other is an inferior being whom I can manipulate to serve my needs, or b) the Other is a superior being, which makes me feel inferior, hence I must either be in service to this superior being, or find the vulnerable spot to launch an attack.

The narcissist cannot comprehend that love can only exist between two equals, two *subjects*, not two *objects*. A narcissist is somebody who was never taught that love is an expression of our essential freedom, not something that can be put in a contract, bought, controlled, or taken by force. Most patients with a narcissistic personality disorder have lived all their life without even one model of a loving relationship; the ecosystems in which they grew up—family, school, culture—had a disturbed balance of exchange, a faulty ecology.

They may have learned to relate to a business partner; they know how to relate to an adversary, to an employee, to the objectified spouse (the spouse as an asset) but they cannot even *imagine* how the beloved is a *spiritual companion*, somebody with whom to feel and create the quality of existence.

Heartbreak, because it breaks the heart open, is the worst offense to whatever amount of narcissism remains in us from infancy—and usually there is *a lot*! It makes heartbreak a most precious occasion to leave behind the conditioning of our culture, which defines love as a commodity, a prize for the successful, something you are entitled to if you are rich or powerful. Being rejected hurts so deeply, it rubs so hard against our natural narcissism, that it can teach us two of the most important lessons about relationships: 1) we don't own the partner because he or she is not an object, and 2) narcissism is a curse, not an advantage over others.

Again, *evolve or perish* is the consistent messages from Nature!

CONCLUSION

Neuroscience is presently one of the most exciting areas in science, one that promises to deliver the cure for such ailments as Alzheimer's disease, autism, schizophrenia, all of which appear related to problematic brain chemistry and neuronal configuration. Nevertheless, as a psychologist, one has to be cautious because these same developments in neuroscience are also responsible for the overmedication of millions of children and adults. Hordes of people are addicted, often from infancy, to drugs to treat ailments that may stem from psycho-cultural problems.

A generation ago, psychology was guilty of suggesting that schizophrenia and autism were the result of faulty mothering. This was a tragic misconception for the many parents who spent their lives trying to adjust their behavior to cure their child, and it created a lot of unnecessary guilt. Schizophrenia and autism, as we now know, are the result of a brain dysfunction, not the result of a psychological trauma.

Today, we are faced with the reverse danger: the medicalization of psycho-cultural diseases. It never was and never will be easy to differentiate a neurobiological problem from one that expresses a cultural or interpersonal dysfunction. As neuroscience itself is demonstrating, the brain emerges from culture and culture emerges from our capacious brains. Big Pharma is always ready to offer medication for whatever can appear as a sickness. Heartbreak is the perfect example of the kind of sickness that calls for explanations from neuroscience, *but also* calls for a revision of our cultural expectations about love and relationships. Both!

Long before neuroscience, it was common knowledge that a child born without hands could be taught to use his toes to accomplish many of the tasks that a person with hands could do, even as we did not know *how* to explain this adaptation. Similarly, we have always known that a blind person will compensate by developing acute hearing. And we have always known that a child deprived of love won't develop. No surprise there!

What neuroscience has contributed is a detailed understanding of *how* something as ethereal and invisible as love, education, art, can actually modify the physical structure of our brains. Neuroscientists are terribly impressed with their discoveries: "Oh wow! Intangible emotions *do* modify the synaptic connections! Wow, meditation calms a nervous mind! Wow, music impacts the neurons! Wow, the ethereal mind can impact the brain."

Their research takes place in labs, most of the time with animals, but more and more with humans. It is done by using Functional Magnetic Resonance Imagery (fMRI), or by slicing dead brains into thin layers to fit under the microscope, or by analyzing the behavior of brain-injured individuals, or by producing new evidence through experimental testing. The scientist works in the lab, the monk meditates, the therapist listens to stories; science is science, meditation is meditation, psychotherapy is psychotherapy.

Yet, these differing approaches share a common fascination with the human potential for either self-healing or self-destruction.[60]

Prudence is part of wisdom

The fact that the brain can be trained is sometimes confused with a kind of New Age trend that borrows ideas from quantum physics and neuroscience, only to create a mythology of unlimited ego power. Scientific discoveries—such as the law of attraction, the plasticity of the brain, or the dual nature of waves and particles—are interpreted to *mean* something that the research is not meant to mean. That *something* is usually an ego-boosting message that caters to a culture of narcissism: "here is the cosmos and here is your marvelous brain. Tap into its power to attract health, wealth, love, success and longevity."

Some, but not all, New Age gurus use words such as evolution, higher consciousness, higher self, visualization, manifestation and positive thinking. It is a sham if they omit the examination of the dark emotions, the regressive pulls, and the discipline needed to obtain results. What these pseudo-gurus are really selling, with great commercial fanfare, is an infantile dream of easy abundance and godlike ego-power. Their relentlessly optimistic suggestion that anybody can access the healing superpower of the brain comes with a view of the cosmos imagined as our own personal playground. It confuses the Self (as Jung understood it) with the ego, and has very little to do with a true process of transformation, and much to do with the consumerist aspect of the culture.

Here, I must add a caveat: first, all those who are now considered New Agers are not necessarily guilty of such inflation; and second, the definition of New Age is often made by the media and is frequently unreliable. For example, an author can be labeled as *New Age* because he or she is interested in the spiritual dimension of the psyche, as Jung was, or because he or she refuses to use jargon and explains things with simplicity, as opposed to simplistic thinking. Jung himself is sometimes considered a New Age author by some of his critics, which reveals a terrible confusion between genres.

The problematic New Agers are those who exclude an examination of the darker aspects of our nature. Jungian psychology, or for that matter, Buddhism, are forms of wisdom that suggest an attitude opposite to New Age self-aggrandizement—an attitude of humility. They both teach that heartbreak makes you a vulnerable, neurotic, pitiful, love-obsessed, defensive, broken human. They suggest that a spiritual journey starts with an honest examination of one's shadow and regressive infantile wishes. The Jungian concept of *individuation*, with its extensive examination of one's hidden darkness, is totally opposed to New Age grandiosity.

A while ago, I sat in an airplane beside a cute six-year-old boy, traveling alone, his name written on an ID card hanging around his neck. He asked me if the plane, since it goes so fast, would soon reach the line that marks the horizon. I would have liked to explain that the horizon is something like perfect love: we keep flying in its direction, but as a final destination, it can never be reached.

Yet without the horizon of love, human life would have no meaning and no sense of direction. I did my best to give the boy as much of a scientific explanation as a six-year-old can grasp: the curvature of the earth, the optical illusion . . . but clearly, it was the experience of this phenomenon which fascinated him, not so much the scientific explanation.

Same for love: neuroscience can *explain* love, but what really fascinates us is the experience, one which needs to be preserved at all costs, above and beyond the pain of heartbreak. That pain turns our inner world into a horrible place, yet it also pushes us out of the limited cage we believed was our love nest.

The brain needs love, and to get that previous invisible substance, we need to become wise humans.

BIBLIOGRAPHY

American Psychiatric Association. (1994). *Diagnostic and statistical manual of mental disorders: DSM-IV.* (4th ed.). Washington, DC: Author.

American Psychiatric Association. (2013). *Diagnostic and statistical manual of mental disorders: DSM-5.* (5th ed.). Washington, DC: Author.

Ainsworth, M. D. S., Blehar, M. C., Waters, E., & Wall, S. (1978). *Patterns of attachment: A psychological study of the strange situation.* Hillsdale, NJ: Lawrence Erlbaum

Ainsworth, M. S. (1979). Infant–mother attachment. *American Psychologist, 34*(10), 932–937. doi:10.1037/0003-066X.34.10.932

Bachelard, G. (1946). *La terre et les rêveries du repos.* Paris, France: Corti.

Bachelard, G. (1971). *The poetics of reverie.* (D. Russell, Trans.). Boston, MA: Beacon Press (Original work published 1960).

Bachelard, G. (2005). *Earth and reveries of repose: An essay on images of interiority.* (M. Jones, Trans.). Dallas, TX: Dallas Institute of Humanities & Culture.

Bachelard, G. (2010). *La poétique de la rêverie.* Paris, France: Presses universitaires de France.

Badenoch, B. (2008). Being a brain-wise therapist: A practical guide to interpersonal neurobiology. New York, NY: Norton.

Beebe, B. (2004). Faces in relation: A case study. *Psychoanalytic Dialogues, 14*(1), 1-51. doi:10.1080/10481881409348771

Beebe, B. (2008). Preface: A relational systems approach to infant research and adult treatment. In L. Carli & C. Rodini (Eds.), *Le forme di intersoggettività: L'implicito e l'esplicito nelle relazioni interpersonali. (Intersubjectivity forms: The implicit and the explicit in the interpersonal relationships*). Milano, Italy: Cortina. Retrieved from http://nyspi.org/

Bekoff, M. (2007). *The emotional lives of animals: A leading scientist explores animal joy, sorrow, and empathy and why they matter.* Novato, CA: New World Library.

Bloom, H. (2000). *How to read and why.* New York, NY: Scribner.

Blakeslee, M. (2002). *In the yikes! zone: A conversation with fear.* New York, NY: Dutton.

Bonanno, G. (2009) *The other side of sadness: What the new science of bereavement tells us about life after loss.* New York, NY: Basic Books

Bonanno, G. A., Coifman, K. G., Ray, R. D., & Gross, J. J. (2007). Does repressive coping promote resilience? Affective-autonomic response discrepancy during bereavement. *Journal of Personality and Social Psychology, 92*(4), 745–758. doi:10.1037/0022-3514.92.4.745

Borofka, D. (2009). *Memory, muses, memoir.* New York, NY: iUniverse.

Bosnak, R. (2007) *Embodiment: Creative imagination in medicine, art and travel.* New York, NY: Routledge.

Bowlby, J. (1980). *Loss: Sadness and depression.* London, England: Hogarth Press.

Bradshaw, G. A., & Schore, A. N. (2007). How elephants are opening doors: Developmental neuroethology, attachment and social context. *Ethology, 113*(5), 426-436. doi:10.1111/j.1439-0310.2007.01333.x

Brown, T. L. (2003). *Making truth: Metaphor in science.* Chicago: University of Illinois Press.

Bruner, J. (1990). *Acts of meaning: Four lectures on mind and culture.* Cambridge, MA: Harvard University Press.

Butler, A. B., & Hodos, W. (2005). *Comparative vertebrate neuroanatomy: Evolution and adaptation* (2nd ed.). Hoboken, NJ: Wiley-Interscience.

Byrne, R. (2006). *The secret*. London, England: Simon & Schuster.

Cabot, C. R., & Reid, J. C. (2001). *Jung, my mother and I: The analytic diaries of Catharine Rush Cabot*. Einsiedeln, Switzerland: Daimon.

Caine, R. N., and Caine, G. (1990). *Making Connections: Teaching and the human brain*. Nashville, TN: Incentive Publications.

Cambray, J. (2002). Synchronicity and emergence. *American Imago, 59*(4), 409-434. doi:10.1353/aim.2002.0023

Cambray, J., & Carter, L. (2004). Analytic methods revisited. In J. Cambray & L. Carter (Eds.), *Analytical psychology: Contemporary perspectives in Jungian analysis* (pp. 116–148). New York, NY: Brunner-Routledge.

Cambray, J. (2009). Nature and Psyche in an Interconnected World. Texas, A&M University Press.

Chua, A., (2011). *The battle hymn of the tiger mother*. London, England: Bloomsbury Press.

Chugani, H. T., Behen, M. E., Muzik, O., Juhász, C., Nagy, F., & Chugani, D. C. (2001). Local brain functional activity following early deprivation: A study of postinstitutionalized Romanian orphans. *NeuroImage, 14*(6), 1290-1301. doi:10.1006/nimg.2001.0917

Comte-Sponville, A. (2002). *Traité du désespoir et de la béatitude*. Paris, France: Presses universitaires de France.

Conforti, M. (2003). *Field, form and fate: Patterns in mind, nature, and psyche.* New Orleans, LA: Spring Journal Books.

Cozolino, L. (2002). *The neuroscience of psychotherapy: Building and rebuilding the human brain.* New York, NY: Norton.

Cozolino, L. (2006). *The neuroscience of human relationships: Attachment and the developing social brain.* New York, NY: Norton.

Crittenden, P. M., & Landini, A. (2011). *The adult attachment interview: Assessing psychological and interpersonal strategies.* New York, NY: Norton.

Cyrulnik, B. (2007). *Talking of love on the edge of a precipice.* London, England: Allen Lane.

Cyrulnik, B. (2009). *Resilience: How your inner strength can set you free from the past.* London, England: Penguin Books.

Damasio, A. (1994). *Descartes' error: Emotion, reason, and the human brain.* New York, NY: Putnam.

Damasio, A. (2003). *Looking for Spinoza: Joy, sorrow, and the human brain.* New York, NY: Harcourt.

Deacon, T. (1997). *The symbolic species: The co-evolution of language and the brain.* New York, NY: Norton.

Downing, C. (Ed.). (1991). *Mirrors of the self: Archetypal images that shape your life.* New York, NY: Tarcher.

Ehrenreich, B. (2009). Bright-sided: How the relentless promotion of positive thinking has undermined America. New York, NY: Metropolitan Books.

George, C., Kaplan, N., & Main, M. (1996). *Adult attachment interview protocol* (3rd ed.). Unpublished manuscript, University of California at Berkeley.

Fonagy, P., Steele, H., & Steele, M. (1991). Maternal representations of attachment during pregnancy predict the organization of infant-mother attachment at one year of age. *Child Development, 62*(5), 891. doi:10.1111/1467-8624.ep9112161635

Fonagy, P., Gergely, G., Jurist, E. L., & Target, M. (2002). *Affect regulation, mentalization, and the development of the self.* London, England: Karnac.

Fonagy, P., & Target, M. (2008). Attachment, trauma, and psychoanalysis: Where psychoanalysis meets neuroscience. In E. L. Jurist, A. Slade, & S. Bergner (Eds.), *Mind to mind: Infant research, neuroscience, and psychoanalysis.* (pp. 15-49). New York, NY: Other Press.

Fukuyama, F. (2011) *The origin of political order from pre-human times to the French Revolution.* New York, N.Y: Farrar, Strauss and Giroux.

Gazzaniga, M. (1998). *The mind's past.* Berkeley: University of California Press.

Gerhardt, S. (2004). *Why love matters: How affection shapes a baby's brain.* New York, NY: Brunner-Routledge.

Gilbert, D. T. (2006). *Stumbling on happiness*. New York, NY: Knopf.

Glenn, D. (2009). A teaching experiment shows students how to grasp big concepts. *Chronicle of Higher Education, 56*(13), A1-A10.

Goodwin, D. (1994). *No ordinary time: Franklin and Eleanor Roosevelt: The home front in World War II*. New York, NY: Simon & Schuster.

Goleman, D. (1996). *Emotional intelligence: Why it can matter more than IQ*. London, England: Bloomsbury Press.

Gould, S. (2007). *Punctuated equilibrium*. Cambridge, MA: Harvard University Press.

Guggenbühl, A. (2009). Love: Our most cherished anarchist, or path to failure? In Riain, S. Wirth, & J. Hill (Eds.), *Intimacy: Venturing the uncertainties of the heart* (pp. 141-152). New Orleans, LA: Spring Journal Books.

Hale, C.A. (2014). *The Red Place: Transforming Past Traumas through Relationships*. London: Muswell Hill Press.

Harrison, R. (2008). *Gardens: An essay on the human condition*. Chicago, IL: University of Chicago Press.

Hawthorne, N. (1850). *The scarlet letter: a romance*. Boston, MA: Ticknor Reed and Fields.

Heilbrun, C. G. (1988). *Writing a woman's life*. New York, NY: Norton

Hennighausen, K., & Lyons-Ruth, K. (2007). Disorganization of attachment strategies in infancy and childhood. In R. Tremblay, R. Barr, R. Peters, & M. Boivin (Eds.), *Encyclopedia on early childhood development* (pp. 1-7). Montreal, Quebec, Canada: Centre of Excellence for Early Childhood Development. Retrieved from http://www.child-encyclopedia.com/documents/Hennighausen-LyonsRuthANGxp_rev.pdf

Hesse, E. (2008). The Adult Attachment Interview: Protocol, method of analysis, and empirical studies. In J. Cassidy & P. R. Shaver (Eds.), *Handbook of attachment: Theory, research, and clinical applications* (2nd ed.). (pp. 552–598). New York, NY: Guilford Press

Hesse, E., & Main, M. (2000). Disorganized infant, child, and adult attachment: Collapse in behavioral and attentional strategies. *Journal of the American Psychoanalytic Association, 48*(4), 1097-1127. doi:10.1177/0003065 1000480041101

Hillman, J. (1964). *Suicide and the soul.* New York, NY: Harper & Row.

Hillman, J. (1972). An essay on Pan. In W. H. Roscher & J. Hillman, *Pan and the nightmare*, (pp. i–lxiii). New York, NY: Spring.

Hillman, J. (1975a). Betrayal. *In Loose ends: Primary papers in archetypal psychology* (pp. 63–81). Dallas, TX: Spring.

Hillman, J. (1975b). *Re-visioning psychology.* New York, NY: Harper & Row.

Hillman, J. (Ed.). (1979). *Puer papers.* Irving, TX: Spring.

Hillman, J. (1989). From mirror to window: Curing psychoanalysis of its narcissism. *Spring Journal, 49,* 62-75.

Hillman, J. (2006). Suicide and the City. In J. Hillman & R. J. Leaver (Ed.), *City & soul* (pp. 116–125). Putnam, CT: Spring Publications

Hillman, J. (2010). *Alchemical psychology.* Putnam, CT: Spring.

Hofer, M. A. (n.d.). Myron Hofer, M.D. - NYSPI Faculty Profiles. Retrieved from http://asp.cumc.columbia.edu/

Hofer, M. A. (1995). An evolutionary perspective on anxiety. In S. P. Roose & R. A. Glick (Eds.), *Anxiety as symptom and signal* (pp. 17-38). Hillsdale, NJ: Analytic Press.

Hofer, M. A., & Sullivan, R. M. (2008). Toward a neurobiology of attachment. In C. A. Nelson & M. Luciana (Eds.), *Handbook of developmental cognitive neuroscience* (2nd ed., pp. 787-805). Cambridge, MA: MIT Press.

Hofstadter, D. R. (2007). *I am a strange loop.* New York, NY: Basic Books

Hogenson, G. B. (2001). The Baldwin effect: A neglected influence on C. G. Jung's evolutionary thinking. *Journal of Analytical Psychology, 46*(4), 591-611. doi:10.1111/1465-5922.00269

Holmes, J. (1996). Attachment, intimacy, autonomy: Using attachment theory in adult psychotherapy. Northvale, NJ: Jason Aronson.

Horney, K. (1939). *New ways in psychoanalysis.* New York, NY: Norton.

Horowitz, M. J., Siegel, B., Holen, A., & Bonanno, G. A. (1997). Diagnostic criteria for complicated grief disorder. *American Journal of Psychiatry, 154*(7), 904–910.

Hutterer, J., & Liss, M. (2006). Cognitive development, memory, trauma, treatment: An integration of psychoanalytic and behavioral concepts in light of current neuroscience research. *Journal of the American Academy of Psychoanalysis & Dynamic Psychiatry, 34*(2), 287-302. doi:10.1521/jaap.2006.34.2.287

Insel, T.R., & Numan, M. (2011) *The Neurobiology of parental behavior.* New York, NY: Springer

Jacobs, W. J. (1983). *Eleanor Roosevelt: A life of happiness and tears.* New York: Coward-McCann.

Jung, C. G. (1967). Symbols of transformation. In H. Read, M. Fordham, G. Adler, & W. McGuire (Eds.), R. F. C. Hull (Trans.), *The collected works of C. G. Jung* (Vol.

5). Princeton, NJ: Princeton University Press (Original work published 1912).

Kalsched, D. (1996). *The inner world of trauma: Archetypal defenses of the personal spirit.* New York, NY: Routledge.

Kandel, E. R. (1998). A new intellectual framework for psychiatry. *American Journal of Psychiatry,* 155(4), 457-469.

Kearney, M. (2000). *A place of healing: Working with suffering in living and dying.* New York, NY: Oxford University Press.

Knox, J. (2003). *Archetype, attachment, analysis: Jungian psychology and the emergent mind.* New York, NY: Brunner-Routledge

Kohut, H. (1966). Forms and transformations of narcissism. *Journal of the American Psychoanalytic Association,* 14(2), 243-272. doi:10.1177/000306516601400201

Kohut, H. (1971). *The analysis of the self: A systematic approach to the psychoanalytic treatment of narcissistic personality disorders.* New York, NY: International Universities Press.

Konigsberg, R. D. (2011). *The truth about grief: The myth of its five stages and the new science of loss.* New York, NY: Simon & Schuster

Konner, M. (1991). Universals of behavioral development in relation to brain myelination. In K. R. Gibson & A. C. Petersen (Eds.), *Brain maturation and cognitive development: Comparative and cross-cultural perspectives.* (pp. 181–223). Hawthorne, NY: Aldine de Gruyter.

Kubler-Ross, E. (1969) *On death and dying.* Simon and Schuster. New York, NY

Lasch, C. (1979). *The culture of narcissism: American life in an age of diminishing expectations.* New York, NY: Warner.

Lane, R. D. (2008). Neural substrates of implicit and explicit emotional processes: A unifying framework for psychosomatic medicine. *Psychosomatic Medicine, 70*(2), 214-231. doi:10.1097/PSY.0b013e3181647e44

LeDoux, J. (1996). The emotional brain: The mysterious underpinnings of emotional life. New York, NY: Simon & Schuster.

LeDoux, J. (2002). *Synaptic self: How our brains become who we are.* New York, NY: Penguin.

Levine, B. E. (2007). *Surviving America's depression epidemic: How to find morale, energy, and community in a world gone crazy.* White River Junction, VT: Chelsea Green

Lewis, T., Amini, F., & Lannon, R. (2000). *A general theory of love.* New York, NY: Random House.

Long, E. (2009). *Metaphor, personification and anthropo-morphization in contemporary popular media repre-sentations of science (Doctoral dissertation).* Pacifica Graduate Institute, Carpinteria, CA. Retrieved from ProQuest Dissertations and Theses database .(1030273595)

Lynch, J. (1977). *The broken heart: The medical consequences of loneliness.* New York, NY: Basic Books.

Lyons-Ruth, K. (1998). Implicit relational knowing: Its role in development and psychoanalytic treatment. *Infant Mental Health Journal, 19*(3), 282-289. doi:10.1002/ (SICI)1097-0355(199823)19:3<282::AID-IMH-J3>3.0.CO;2-O

Lyons-Ruth, K. (1999). The two-person unconscious: Inter-subjective dialogue, enactive relational representa-tion, and the emergence of new forms of relational organization. *Psychoanalytic Inquiry, 19*(4), 576-617. doi:10.1080/07351699909534267

Mahaffey, P. (2005). Jung's depth psychology and yoga sadha-na. In K. Jacobsen (Ed.), *Theory and practice of yoga: Essays in honour of Gerald James Larson* (pp. 385-408). Leiden, Netherlands: Brill.

Main, M., Kaplan, N., & Cassidy, J. (1985). Security in in-fancy, childhood, and adulthood: A move to the level of representation. In I. Bretherton & E. Waters (Eds.), *Growing points of attachment theory and research* (pp. 66–104). Chicago, IL: University of Chicago Press

Mancia, M. (2006). Implicit memory and early unrepressed unconscious: Their role in the therapeutic process (How the neurosciences can contribute to psychoanalysis). *International Journal of Psycho-Analysis, 87*(1), 83-103.

Mar, R. A. (2004). The neuropsychology of narrative: Story comprehension, story production and their interrelation. *Neuropsychologia, 42*(10), 1414-1434. doi:10.1016/j.neuropsychologia.2003.12.016

Marlan, S. (2005). *The black sun: The alchemy and art of darkness.* College Station: Texas A & M University Press.

Masterson, J. F. (1993). The emerging self: A developmental, self, and object relations approach to the treatment of the closet narcissistic disorder of the self. New York, NY: Brunner/Mazel

McGilchrist, I. (2009). The master and his emissary: The divided brain and the making of the Western world. New Haven, CT: Yale University Press.

McKinney, W. T. (2000). Animal research and its relevance to psychiatry. In B. J. Sadock & V. A. Sadock (Eds.), *Kaplan & Sadock's comprehensive textbook of psychiatry* (7th ed., pp. 545–562). Philadelphia, PA: Lippincott Williams & Wilkins.

Melville, H. (1851). *Moby-Dick or, The whale.* New York, NY: Harper.

Michaux, H. (1963). *Passages 1937-1963.* Nouvelle édition revue et augmentée. Paris, France: Gallimard.

Miller, A. (1981). *The drama of the gifted child.* New York, NY: Basic Books.

Miller, D. (1995). Nothing almost sees miracles! Self and no-Self in psychology and religion. *Journal of the Psychology of Religion, 4-5,* 1-26.

Miller, D. (2005). *Three faces of God: Traces of the Trinity in literature and life* (New ed.). New Orleans, LA: Spring Journal Books. (Original work published 1986)

Millon, T. (2004). *Personality disorders in modern life* (2nd ed.). Hoboken, NJ: Wiley.

Modell, A. H. (1997). The synergy of memory, affects and metaphor. *Journal of Analytical Psychology, 42*(1), 105-117.

Murdock, M. (2003). *Unreliable truth: On memoir and memory.* New York, NY: Seal Press.

Offer, M. (1995). An evolutionary perspective on anxiety. In S. Roose (Ed.), *Anxiety as symptom and signal* (pp. 25-27). Hillsdale, NJ: Analytic Press.

Panksepp, J. (1998). Affective neuroscience: The foundations of human and animal emotions. New York, NY: Oxford University Press.

Panksepp, J. (2003). At the interface of the affective, behavioral, and cognitive neurosciences: Decoding the emotional feelings of the brain. *Brain and Cognition, 52*(1), 4-14. doi:10.1016/S0278-2626(03)00003-4

Panksepp, J., (Ed.) (2004) *A Textbook of Biological Psychiatry*. New York, NY: Wiley

Panksepp, J. (2008). The power of the word may reside in the power of affect. *Integrative Psychological & Behavioral Science, 42*(1), 47-55. doi:10.1007/s12124-007-9036-5

Paris, G. (2007). Wisdom of the psyche: Depth psychology after neuroscience. New York, NY: Routledge.

Pearson, C. (1986). *The hero within: Six archetypes we live by*. San Francisco, CA: Harper & Row.

Phillips, A. (1994). *On flirtation*. Cambridge, MA: Harvard University Press.

Phillips, A. (2005). *Going sane: Maps of happiness*. New York, NY: HarperCollins.

Prasad, A. (2007). Apical ballooning syndrome: An important differential diagnosis of acute myocardial infarction. *Circulation, 115*(5), e56–e59. doi:10.1161/CIRCULATIONAHA.106.669341

Prins, A., Kaloupek, D. G., & Keane, T. M. (1995). Psychophysiological evidence for autonomic arousal and startle in traumatized adult populations. In M. J. Friedman,

D. S. Charney, & A. Y. Deutch (Eds.), *Neurobiological and clinical consequences of stress: From normal adaptation to post-traumatic stress disorder.* (pp. 291-314). Philadelphia, PA: Lippincott-Raven.

Proust, M. (1996). *La fin de la jalousie: Et autres nouvelles.* Paris, France: Gallimard. (Original work published 1923)

Proust, M. (1954). *A la recherche du temps perdu.* Paris, France: Gallimard.

Proust, M. (1990). *Le temps retrouvé.* Paris, France: Gallimard. (Original work published 1927)

Ratey, J. J. (2002). A user's guide to the brain: Perception, attention and the four theaters of the brain. New York, NY: Vintage Books.

Reid, J. C., & Cabot, C. R. (2001). *Jung, my mother and I: The analytic diaries of Catharine Rush Cabot.* Einsiedeln, Switzerland: Daimon

Roose, S. (1995). *Anxiety as symptom and signal.* Hillsdale, NJ: Analytic Press.

Rossi, E. L. (2007). The breakout heuristic: The neuroscience of mirror neurons, consciousness and human creativity. Phoenix, AZ: Milton Erickson Foundation Press.

Rowland, S. (2002). *Jung: A feminist revision.* Malden, MA: Blackwell.

Rowland, S. (2005). *Jung as a writer*. New York, NY: Routledge.

Russell. F., (1993) *Eleanor Roosevelt: A Life of Discovery*. New York, NY: Clarion Books.

Sander, L. (1977). The regulation of exchange in the infant caretaker system and some aspects of the context-content relationship. In M. Lewis & L. Rosenblum (Eds.), *Interaction, conversation, and the development of language* (pp. 133-156). New York, NY: Wiley.

Sander, L. W. (2002). Thinking differently: Principles of process in living systems and the specificity of being known. *Psychoanalytic Dialogues, 12*(1), 11-42. doi:10.1080/10481881209348652

Schoen, D. (2009). The war of the gods in addiction: C.G. Jung, Alcoholics Anonymous, and archetypal evil. New Orleans, LA: Spring Journal Books.

Schwartz-Salant, N. (2007). The black nightgown: The fusional complex and the unlived life. Wilmette, IL: Chiron.

Schore, A. N. (2002). Dysregulation of the right brain: A fundamental mechanism of traumatic attachment and the psychopathogenesis of posttraumatic stress disorder. *Australian and New Zealand Journal of Psychiatry, 36*(1), 9-30. doi:10.1046/j.1440-1614.2002.00996.x

Schore, A. N. (2003). *Affect regulation and the repair of the self*. New York, NY: Norton.

Schore, A. N. (2003b). *Affect dysregulation and disorders of the self.* New York, NY: Norton.

Schore, A. N. (2008). Paradigm shift: The right brain and the relational unconscious. *Psychologist-Psychoanalyst, 28*(3), 20–25.

Schore, A. N. (2012). *The science of the art of psychotherapy.* New York, NY: Norton

Schore, J. R., & Schore, A. N. (2008). Modern attachment theory: The central role of affect regulation in development and treatment. *Clinical Social Work Journal, 36*(1), 9-20. doi:10.1007/s10615-007-0111-7

Sharp, D. (1991). *Jung lexicon: A primer of terms and concepts.* Toronto, Canada: Inner City Books.

Siegel, D. (1999). The developing mind: Toward a neurobiology of interpersonal experience. New York, NY: Guilford Press.

Siegel, D. (2007). The mindful brain: Reflection and attunement in the cultivation of well-being. New York, NY: Norton

Siegel, D. (2009). The healing power of emotion: Affective neuroscience, development & clinical practice. New York, NY: Norton.

Siegel, D. (2010). The mindful therapist: A clinician's guide to mindsight and neural integration. New York, NY: Norton.

Siegel, D. & Solomon, M. F. (Eds.). (2003). *Healing Trauma: Attachment, mind, body and brain.* New York, NY: Norton.

Solms, M. (2002). The brain and the inner world: An introduction to the neuroscience of subjective experience. New York, NY: Other Press

Somerville, M. (1996). *Eleanor Roosevelt As I Knew Her.* McLean, VA: EPM.

Spiegel, J., Severino, S. K., & Morrison, N. K. (2000). The role of attachment functions in psychotherapy. *Journal of Psychotherapy Practice & Research, 9*(1), 25–32

Stark, M. (1999). Modes of therapeutic action: Enhancement of knowledge, provision of experience, and engagement in relationship. Northvale, NJ: Jason Aronson..

Stein, M. (1998). *Jung's map of the soul: An introduction.* Chicago, IL: Open Court.

Stein, M. (2006). Individuation. In R. K. Papadopoulos (Ed.), *The handbook of Jungian psychology: Theory, practice and applications.* (pp. 196-214). New York, NY: Routledge.

Stern, D., Sander, L., Nahum, J., Harrison, A., Lyons-Ruth, K., Morgan, A., Bruschweilerstern, N., et al. (1998). Non-interpretive mechanisms in psychoanalytic therapy: The 'something more' than interpretation. *The International Journal of Psychoanalysis, 79*(5), 903-921.

Stern, D. (2004). The present moment in psychotherapy and everyday life. New York, NY: Norton.

Stewart, C. (2008). Dire emotions and lethal behaviors: Eclipse of the life instinct. New York, NY: Routledge.

Tacy, D. (2004). The Spirituality Revolution: The Emergence of contemporary spirituality. New York, NY: Routledge.

Tallis, R. (2011). Aping mankind: Neuromania, Darwinitis and the misrepresentation of humanity. Durham, England: Acumen.

Taylor, J. B. (2006). My stroke of insight: A brain scientist's personal journey. New York, NY: Viking.

Taylor, S. E., Klein, L. C., Lewis, B. P., Gruenewald, T. L., Gurung, R. A. R., & Updegraff, J. A. (2000). Biobehavioral responses to stress in females: Tend-and-befriend, not fight-or-flight. *Psychological Review, 107*(3), 411-429. doi:10.1037/0033-295X.107.3.411

Tronick, E. (2007). The neurobehavioral and social-emotional development of infants and children. New York, NY: Norton.

Tulving, E., & Craik, F. I. M. (Eds.). (2000). *The Oxford handbook of memory*. New York, NY: Oxford University Press.

Turbayne, C. (1971). *The myth of metaphor* (Rev. ed.). Columbia: University of South Carolina Press.

Twenge, J., & Campbell, W. K. (2009). *The narcissism epidemic: Living in the age of entitlement.* New York, NY: Free Press.

Verplaetse, J., Braeckman, J., De Schrijver, J., & Vanneste, S. (Eds.). (2009). *The moral brain: Essays on the evolutionary and neuroscientific aspects of morality.* New York, NY: Springer.

Von Franz, M.-L. (1981). *Puer aeternus* (2nd ed.). Santa Monica, CA: Sigo Press

Youngs, J. W T. (2006). *Eleanor Roosevelt: A personal and public life.* (M. C. Carnes, Ed.) (3rd ed.). New York, NY: Pearson/Longman

Watt, D. F. (2004). Psychotherapy in an age of neuroscience. In J. Corrigall & H. Wilkinson (Eds.), *Revolutionary connections: Psychotherapy and neuroscience* (pp. 79-115). New York, NY: Karnac.

Watt, D. F. (2005). Social bonds and the nature of empathy. *Journal of Consciousness Studies, Emotion experience, 12*(8-10), 185-209.

Wheeler, M. A. (2000). Episodic memory and autonoetic awareness. In E. Tulving & F. I. M. Craik (Eds.), *The Oxford handbook of memory.* (pp. 597–608). New York, NY: Oxford University Press

Whitaker, R. (2010). Anatomy of an epidemic: Magic bullets, psychiatric drugs, and the astonishing rise of mental illness in America. New York, NY: Crown Publishers

Wilkinson, M. (2003). Undoing trauma: Contemporary neuroscience. A Jungian clinical perspective. *Journal of Analytical Psychology, 48*(2), 235-253.

Wilkinson, M. (2004). The mind-brain relationship: The emergent self. *Journal of Analytical Psychology, 49*(1), 83-101. doi:10.1111/j.0021-8774.2004.0442.x

Wilkinson, M. (2006). Coming into mind: The main-brain relationship: A Jungian clinical perspective. London, England: Routledge.

Wilkinson, M. (2007a). Jung and neuroscience: The making of mind. In A. Casement (Ed.), *Who owns Jung?* (pp. 339-362). London, England: Karnac Books.

Wilkinson, M. (2007b). Coming into mind: Contemporary neuroscience, attachment, and the psychological therapies: A clinical perspective. *Attachment: New directions in psychotherapy and relational psychoanalysis, 1*(3), 323-330.

Wilkinson, M. (2010). Changing minds in therapy: emotion, attachment, trauma, and neurobiology. New York, NY: Norton.

Wilson, E. O. (1998). *Consilience: The unity of knowledge.* New York, NY: Knopf.

Young, K., & Saver, J. L. (2001). The Neurology of Narrative. *SubStance, 30*(1), 72-84. doi:10.1353/sub.2001.0020

Zweig, C., & Wolf, S. (1997). *Romancing the shadow: Illuminating the dark side of the soul*. New York, NY: Ballantine Books

Zoja, L. (2010). Carl Gustav Jung as a historical–cultural phenomenon. *International Journal of Jungian Studies*, 2(2), 141–150. doi:10.1080/19409052.2010.507995

ENDNOTES

1 "Quant au bonheur, il n'a presque qu'une seule utilité, rendre le malheur possible. Il faut que dans le bonheur nous formions des liens bien doux et bien forts de confiance et d'attachement pour que leur rupture nous cause le déchirement si précieux qui s'appelle le malheur. Si l'on n'avait pas été heureux, ne fût-ce que par l'espérance, les malheurs seraient sans cruauté et par conséquent sans fruit.» Proust (1927/1990, p. 907). My translation.

2 Hillman (1975b, p. 66).

3 Solms.

4 As Panksepp (1998) writes : "This three-layered conceptualization helps us grasp the overall function of higher brain areas better than any other scheme yet devised. Of course, exceptions can be found to all generalizations, and it must be kept in mind that the brain is a massively interconnected organ whose every part can find an access pathway to any other part. Even though many specialists have criticized the overall accuracy of the image of a 'triune brain', the conceptualization provides a useful overview of mammalian brain organization above the lower brain stem (p. 70) [. . .] Paul MacLean's triune brain concept is supported by a variety of observations. Although a debatable simplification from a strictly neuroanatomical perspective, MacLean's formulation provides a clear

and straightforward way to begin conceptualizing the brain's overall organization" (p. 61).

A number of experts, among whom are Konner (1991) and McKinney (2000), have recognized that the three layers of the brain and their associated behavioral complexes do exist in the brain, although again, specialized research now uses more detailed maps than this rough division of the brain into three layers of evolution. Today those who refer to MacLean's theory use it not so much to discuss where the human brain falls on the scale of evolutionary progress, but rather to discuss which selective forces in the culture can shape it.

5 "[. . .] the critical weakness of MacLean's model is his description of brain evolution as a ladder like process of progressive change and his invocation of three directional evolution, views that are inconsistent with modern understandings of the evolutionary process" (Butler and Hodos, 1996).

6 As Butler and Hodos argue, (2005, p. 116) argue, MacLean's optimism was reminiscent of the now discredited 'predetermined path' theory of orthogenesis, where humans will inevitably come closer to God. Neuroscience clearly demonstrates how adaptation can be a regressive one, a fact that is more frequent than we would like to believe.

7 Caine et al. (1990).

8 Melville (1851, Chapter 44).

9 The work of Joseph Ledoux (1996 and 2002) clarified the function of the amygdala in stocking our memories; he demonstrated how, along with the amygdala's central role, the whole brain is involved.

10 This one from Elvis!

11   Given the long history and fierce theoretical debates around the use of the word *unconscious*, neuroscientists and

neuro-psychologists have been quick to take their distance from the psychoanalytic tradition and usually prefer to use their own terms. Allan Schore for example, prefers to use *non-conscious memories* to avoid calling them *unconscious*. His makes a contrast between something that is unconscious because it was once known and repressed, (the Freudian concept of the unconscious as a *repressed* memory) which is very different from memory that is non-conscious because it was either *implicit* from the beginning, or because one *dissociated* from it because it was too painful which is closer to a Jungian sense of unconsciousness.

Cognitive neuroscientists prefer the word *implicit* memory or *procedural memory*, a form of memory that is there from birth: the baby picks a blueberry, bring it to his mouth and never forgets where his mouth is. (Same as riding a bicycle.) Implicit memory or procedural memories are opposed to *explicit* memory, specific to humans, which requires verbal capacity and a conscious, *autobiographical* memory: "look mommy, I ate all the blueberries"

12 See: Bekoff (2007).

13 See: Lynch (1977).

14 Researchers at The Sackler Institute for Developmental Psychobiology at the Columbia University College of Physicians and Surgeons have developed ways of appraising how, in laboratory rats, early maternal separation affects the offspring's vulnerability to disease. They have confirmed many of the regulatory processes that were at the level of hypothesis in psychological theories of attachment. Their research offers a neurological basis for understanding the damage that results from a traumatic separation from the usual caregivers or partners, and the impact it has at the molecular, cellular, behavioral, and psychological levels.

160   *Heartbreak, Mourning, Loss*

15 Mary Ainsworth et al. (1978).

16 Attachment theory was developed in the 1950's by psychologists John Bowlby and later by Mary Ainsworth who examined four attachment strategies: 1. Secure attachment: you show interest and affection but are also comfortable being alone and independent. 2. Anxious: you are nervous about relationships, you need constant reassurance and affection from the partner. 3. Avoidant: You are uncomfortable with intimacy, easily feel the other is invasive, and you are a champion at exit strategies like busyness and workaholism, or collecting lovers. 4. Anxious-avoidant: you are afraid of intimacy but still you seem to never get enough of it. When you get it, you lash out at the partner who tries to get close to you. You end up isolated and miserable, or in abusive or dysfunctional relationships like you experienced in childhood.

The difficulty with such neat categories is that it tends to be interpreted as fate: "this is who I am". But as we now know, the attachment style will change if one becomes more conscious, for example through the process of therapy, or what Jungians call individuation. The personality of the partner is also a important factor: one can "move up" to become more secure, or regress to a level of insecurity if the partner repeatedly destroys your sense of security. And of course, traumatic life events will cause even a secure attachment type to regress to insecure attachment style of relating.

17 Lewis, Amini, & Lannon (2000, p. 79).

18 See: (Beebee 2008; Tronick 2007; Stern et al. 1998) See also Ainsworth (1979) and *The Adult Attachment Interview* as developed by Main, Kaplan, & Cassiby (1985) and discussed in Crittenden (2011).

19 See Kalsched (1996).

20 The French psychiatrist BorisCyrulnik (2009) who worked with war orphans explains what makes some individual more resilient than others.

21 American Psychiatric Association (1994).

22 Prasad (2007). See also information on broken heart syndrome as well as cardiomyopathy offered on the website of the Division of Cardiovascular Diseases and Department of Internal Medicine, Mayo Clinic and Mayo Foundation. http://www.mayoclinic.org

23 For more information, see also the website: http://www.hopkinsmedicine.org/asc/

24 Whitaker 2010; Levine 2007. See also: *Psychiatry Now Admits It's Been Wrong in Big Ways - But Can It Change?* On the website: truth-out.org

25 See James Hillman's discussion of masturbation in *"An essay on Pan"* (1972). He concludes the chapter with this thought: "Because it is the only sexual activity performed alone, we may not judge it solely in terms of its service to the species or to society. Rather than focusing upon its useless role in external civilization and procreation, we may reflect upon its usefulness for internal culture and creativity. By intensifying interiority with joy—and with conflict and shame, and by vivifying fantasy, masturbation, which has no purpose for species or society, yet brings genital pleasure, fantasy and guilt to the individual as psychic subject. It sexualizes fantasy, brings body to mind, intensifies the experience of conscience and confirms the powerful reality of the introverted psyche— was it not invented for the solitary shepherd piping through the empty places of our inscapes and who re-appears when we are thrown into solitude. By constellating Pan, masturbation brings nature and its complexity back into the *opus contra naturam* of soul-making" (p. xxxv).

26 Taylor et al. (2000).

27 Phillips (1994, p. xviii).

28 What is this denial between humans and animals actually doing? Tallis writes: "Neuromania and Darwinitis leave little or no room for human freedom. If we are identical with our brains, and our brains are evolved organs, how can we do anything other than act out a preordained evolutionary script?" Tallis's philosophical argument is based on the fact that a brain scan reveals a mere correlation, not causation. An fMRI will reveal what area of my brain lights-up when I (or a rat) eat chocolate, but that does not define the essence of pleasure, happiness, and joy for us humans.

29 Hofstadter (2007).

30 Stan Marlan (2005, p. 27).

31 Jung (1967, p. 357).

32 As Wheeler notes, "the retrieval of episodic information [...] is not merely an objective account of what has happened or what has been seen or heard. Its contents are infused with the idiosyncratic perspectives, emotions, and thoughts of the person doing the remembering. It necessarily involves the feeling that the present recollection is a re-experience of something that has happened before" (2000, p. 597). The author also mentions how the act of recollecting and reflecting upon one's past is cognitively and neurologically similar to the act of anticipating one's future, although we don't use the word memory in that case. By contrast to the autonoetic memory, a noetic (knowing) memory is one where we don't need to recall or relive the past to remember something that has become a routine, like reaching for your wallet in the back pocket. (p. 598).

33 Wheeler (2000, p. 598).

34 One should not confuse implicit memory with procedural memory. Most of our daily routine is accomplished without conscious control. A routine stems from what neuroscientists call the *procedural memory*. For example, driving home in your car does not demand that you be conscious of every turn you take to navigate your way home. You find your way like a horse returning to the stable.

35 Schore (2012).

36 Bachelard (1946, p. 28). My translation

37 Neurons either thrive when connected in circuit with other neurons, or they die when they sit in isolation without stimulation. Taylor (2006, p. 97).

38 Cyrulnick (2009).

39 In evolutionary biology, this capacity to adapt is called by Stephen Jay Gould and Niles Eldridge 'punctuated equilibrium' in opposition to Darwin's 'gradualism'. (Gould, 2007).

40 Panksepp (1998, p. 16).

41 Schore (2003).

42 My father was an electrical contractor; my first stack of metaphors to understand the psyche were those of shorts, overloaded circuits, power failures, power differential, power shortages, shock and electrocution. I was impressed by the beautiful complexity of blueprints showing the inner wiring of a big building such as a school or a hospital and equally impressed by my father's uncanny ability to figure out, better than any engineer on site, any mistake in a blueprint. Seeing him at work was my first exposure to the glory of rational thinking. He is one of my welcome ghosts, a provider of metaphors. My repertoire has since expanded: the whole sensate reality is a repertoire of embodied metaphors to pick and choose from.

43 See:Verplaetse, Braeckman, De Schrijver, & Vanneste (2009). Although most scientists discredited the idea of a *moral organ* as phrenologists once did, there is new emerging evidence that specific brain processes enable moral cognition.

44 Jung (as cited in Sharp, 1991, p. 72).

45 See: Schoen (2009).

46 Lasch (1979).

47 It might be useful to examine borderline traits as narcissistic traits and vice versa, especially when it comes to the notion of 'lack of empathy'. Although the narcissist has a more stable self-image and less self-destructiveness, both the narcissist and the borderline personality lack empathy for the other.

48 Kohut (1971 and 1966).

49 Horney (1939).

50 Masterson (1993).

51 Millon (2004).

52 Twenge & Campbell (2009).

53 Hillman (1989, pp. 62-75).

54 Twenge & Campbell (2009).

55 There are no less than 36,000 different credits cards available to a US citizen as compared to 400 in Canada. This number comprises all the major ones, like Visa, Master Card or American Express, but we tend to forget that companies like Esso, Home Depot, Sears, Amazon...all offer their own brand of credit cards. The total of individual credit cards in circulation in the US was 1.3 billion at the end of 2003, U.S. compared to 9 million in France. (The French and the German use mostly debit cards). See regular information about credit card debt in the industry newsletter the Nilson Report. Also: www.creditcards.com for detailed statistics.

56 Twenge & Campbell (2009).

57 Franz (1981).

58 Goodwin, in *No Ordinary Time* (1994), wrote how, during the depression and World War II, Eleanor traveled throughout the country, bringing reports back to FDR.

59 David Miller, a theologian, formulates the idea this way: "The majority of mystical theologies in the world's religious traditions hold as a spiritual goal precisely the nothingness and emptiness about which those who suffer today complain. The spiritual goal in these religious traditions is spoken of in a rhetoric that suggests that one should not aspire to achieve self-sense, self-hood, or identity, but that one precisely loose these in favor of a sense of no-self". (1995-1996, p. 4).

60 "We can now conceptualize basic psychological processes in neurological terms that appeared terminally stuck in unproductive semantic realms only a few years ago. Neuroscientific riches are now so vast that all subfields of psychology must begin to integrate a new and strange landscape into their thinking if they want to stay on the forefront of scientific inquiry. This new knowledge will have great power to affect human welfare, as well as human self-conception. It is finally possible to credibly infer the natural order of the 'inner causes' of behavior, including the emotional process that activate many of the coherent psycho-behavioral tendencies animals and humans exhibit spontaneously without much prior learning. These natural brain processes help create the deeply felt value structures that govern much of our behavior, whether learned or unlearned. This new mode of thought is the intellectual force behind affective neuroscience" Panksepp (1998, p. 11).

TABLE OF CONTENTS OF VOLUME 1
HEARTBREAK, MOURNING, LOSS
DETACH OR DIE

www.ingramcontent.com/pod-product-compliance
Lightning Source LLC
Chambersburg PA
CBHW021336290326
41933CB00038B/780